ARE YOU HAUNTED BY THE FACT THAT YOU'RE

WORKING HARD
AND EARNING MONEY,
BUT NOT SAVING ENOUGH,
IF ANYTHING AT ALL?

Does retiring with a few million bucks in the bank seem like something that only other people can do, but not you? It's time to listen to that voice inside of you that knows you can do better than what you're doing now. This book is here to show you how.

Unlike other personal finance books that hand down advice from a high lofty perch, advisor and entrepreneur Kevin Frisbie offers a warm and trustworthy hand to personally guide you from wherever it is you happen to be now, to a place of financial security. His down-to-earth manner and inspiring true story give us living proof that a person can come from a disadvantaged background, make the worst mistakes possible, have terrible timing, and still amass a fortune. This is more than just a book about how and in what to invest; this is a process, a habit, and a way of life.

WELCOME TO
EVERY DIME, EVERY DAY.

A special thanks goes out to my wife Erika who has worked hard, watched, and supported this whole process from a 1 bedroom efficiency apartment to the amazing life we live today

A thank you to our son Mitchel who also has watched over the years and sometimes didn't understand our focus and goals that we work so hard to achieve. He has enjoyed the fruits of our work from traveling to many foreign countries, warm beach resorts and countless times to Disney Parks. Mitchel you are now a young adult and we can only hope that you carry on the legacy that we have built and live your own life with the example we have set out before you.

A thank you to my family and friends, my parents and uncle Benny who continue to cheer me on to reach new heights

To all of my mentors including John Jamison who believed in a broken and broke Kevin Frisbie so much that he took me under his wing to teach me and guide me to some of the lessons that were so critical for our success.

Lastly, a huge thank you to my current and future clients for allowing us to be your guides to and through retirement.

EVERY DIME, EVERY DAY

A LIFE-CHANGING PERSONAL FINANCE PLAN CREATED TO TAKE YOU FROM WHERE YOU ARE TODAY

TO WHEREVER IT IS YOU WANT TO GO.

KEVIN FRISBIE

Financial Advisor & Entrepreneur

CONTENTS

A BOY, A JEEP, AND A CHANGE
FOR THE BETTER

We cannot solve our problems with the same
thinking we used to create them.

~ Albert Einstein

My downfall came in the form of four doors, a step-up bar, and a soft top. It was an unbelievably beautiful Jeep, and I'll never forget the first time I saw it sitting there in the middle of a showroom in Augusta, Maine. Even though it was way more than I could afford, even though I had no business buying a new vehicle and didn't even come there looking for a Jeep, I absolutely had to have it. I thought I deserved a more exciting ride because I was working hard and earning money. It was an impulse buy, a spur-of-the-moment decision, and it felt great driving that Jeep off the lot.

It felt great, until things came crashing down during the summer of 1992. I lost my job, my apartment, and my ability to afford the payments for my Jeep. I remember very clearly sitting in the backseat of my parents' car with my forehead pressed against the window glass. I was 21 years old at the time and at the low point of my life thus far.

My nose made little plumes of fog as hot tears rolled down my face. My mom drove us away, and I watched through the window as my Jeep sitting there in a repo lot got smaller and smaller. I never saw that Jeep again, and that moment forever changed my life. It was the beginning of *Every Dime, Every Day*.

As you read this, wherever you are at in your life, however high your debt, however low your hope, think about where you've come from and the financial decisions you've made up to this point. Understand that you made each decision to the best of your ability, based on who you were and what you knew at that time. Understand that you don't have to keep making these same decisions, these same mistakes. You can learn how to make new decisions. You can choose to do something different. You can change. This book is here to show you how.

SO THIS IS WHERE YOU ARE, BUT WHERE DO YOU WANT TO GO?

Success is a learned behavior, and if you haven't experienced it yet in the area of finances, then it's simply because you haven't developed the right habits. I'm here as living proof that a person can come from a disadvantaged background, make the worst mistakes possible, have terrible timing, and still amass a fortune. I did it by following a simple process I call, *Every Dime, Every Day*.

My story began before I was even born, when my biological father tried to kill me while my mother was pregnant. In spite of his efforts, I survived and came into this world.

Our family came from a small town, and we lived a lower-middle-class existence. My mother and eventually my stepfather (who was kind and treated me like his own son) taught me about hard work. From their example I learned how to make money by exchanging hours for dollars. I just didn't know what, exactly, to do with those dollars.

So, I did what any good citizen would do: I spent them! Worse than that, I spent more dollars than I made. In my mind, I wasn't being extravagant at all. I spent money in very common ways, American ways. I worked hard, and so I thought that meant I deserved nice things. I looked at my earnings and what I felt like I could afford, and I went out and bought a new car because, at the time, I didn't understand the true meaning of the word "afford."

The summer I lost my Jeep, I learned that there are two kinds of pride. There's the kind that hurts, that makes you think you're better than you really are, and then there's the kind of pride that takes joy in doing and being the best you can be. This second kind of pride also takes joy in seeing people you care about achieve success, and I like to think it was that second kind of pride that helped me out the day I gave up my Jeep. It made me too proud to allow my car to be repossessed in my parents' driveway, made me ask them for help. They followed me to the repo lot where I turned in my Jeep and my keys, and faced the consequences of my choices. And it made me think, in the backseat of their car, *I know I can do better than this; I just need to figure out how.*

This book is the culmination of what I've learned, and I'm calling on the better side of your pride now as you read this.

If you grow anxious every time you open the mail, if you have more bills, more debt, more student loans, car loans, mortgages, or debt of any kind than you can handle, and you're sick of worrying and working hard just to pay it off, you certainly aren't alone. And you aren't without hope. If you know you can do better than you're doing now, if you've been trying to figure out how, this book was written to help. It's a tool that can show you how to go from wherever it is you are today, to wherever it is you want to be. This isn't a gimmick or a trick or an easy way out. It's a process, a habit, and a way of life.

Welcome to *Every Dime, Every Day*. This is a life-changing personal finance plan that I created based on my own experiences with debt. It is the product of all the books, seminars, and information I gathered and absorbed during my quest for a better life. If you're not where you want to be financially, then you've come to right place, and what's more, you've come at the right time. You see, change is hard. Making real and permanent change often involves some pretty uncomfortable steps, and that's why this book is here.

To take the first step, you'll need three things: a plan to fix the things that aren't working, a genuine motivation to get working on the plan, and a financial professional in your corner to coach you through it all. Luckily for you, this book has all three.

HOW TO USE THIS BOOK

Because true transformation is a process, that's exactly what this book presents. I've broken the *Every Dime, Every Day* process into specific, strategic concepts and steps. Each chapter shows you the ins and outs of a concept and includes a series of steps to take before moving on.

The "before moving on" part is important. There might be steps that take a few weeks of practice, or even a few months. Take the logbook, for example. You'll get to that in Chapter 4. The logbook is the foundation of *Every Dime, Every Day*, and it's a big, new habit you'll have to form. It involves collecting receipts for every purchase you make—even if it's just a pack of gum at the gas station—and then recording them at the end of each day.

If you're anything like me, you'll forget to ask for receipts. You'll lose receipts. You'll get busy and not record your receipts for a day or two. Today, I'm diligent about every part of the logbook, but it wasn't always that way. Even though I invented the logbook for myself, I still had a hard time getting it perfect for a while. It took me months to get the logbook habit down.

So, the first rule of *Every Dime, Every Day*: Be patient with yourself.

The second rule is—to borrow from Winston Churchill—Never, ever, ever give up.

And that's it. Read through the chapters, and work through the steps. Accept that you'll have slip-ups, mistakes, and setbacks, but don't let them get you off course. If you do those things, you will be able to achieve your financial goals, and once you do that, all kinds of other dreams become possible.

I became a financial professional because I have seen, firsthand, the results of having a solid game plan, and how achieving financial freedom can transform your life and the lives of those around you. Imagine saying goodbye forever to all of your debt. Imagine leaving behind all that stress you're carrying around right now. Imagine knowing, deep in your heart, that whatever dreams you have, you will be able to make them realities.

You can. *Every Dime, Every Day* will show you how. I'm glad you're here.

All my best,

Kevin Frisbie

Chapter 1:
LEARNING TO WORK VS.
LEARNING TO SUCCEED

Knowing is not enough; we must apply. Willing is not enough; we must do.

~ Johann Wolfgang von Goethe

The years from 1992 to 2000 were a long, hard road, but finally I felt like I was headed in the right direction. This was one of the highpoints of my life. My wife and I had been working, sometimes two jobs, paying down debt and even saving. We had a baby, and my wife stayed home with our son while I worked a manufacturing job. We both kept a tight rein on our finances, we continued to save, and we dreamed big. We even took a video of that small apartment with its broken TV, empty fridge, and leaky waterbed, joking at the time that "this is where it all starts." That's how it all began: by dreaming and jokingly videotaping.

By 2001, we'd amassed what felt to us like a small fortune: $27,314. We decided that now was the time to invest our savings, to use the stock market to turn all our hard work around and make it work for us.

On Sept. 10, 2001, we invested every cent of our savings into the stock market.

I was working late nights then, and I didn't get home until 6:30 in the morning on Sept. 11. I was too excited to sleep very long. We were now officially investors, and I couldn't wait to see how our investments were faring. We'd selected three tech companies to invest in, and it was thrilling to think about what our stocks were posting at on our very first day as investors.

I poured a cup of coffee, sat down at my computer, and waited for the markets to open. But nothing happened. What day was it? I checked the calendar. Tuesday. *Something should happen any time now.* But nothing changed. I kept refreshing and refreshing the screen, but no stocks were moving. That was when I flipped on the television and saw the planes that had hit the Twin Towers.

I called my wife Erika and told her to come home. She had once lived in Manhattan, and we had many friends who still did. I knew we needed to be together.

That day was a tragedy, and our small loss does not at all compare to the unimaginable devastation so many people faced and are still feeling today. Nevertheless, we came out of that experience and it felt like we were back to square one. We had lost a huge chunk of our savings, enough that we certainly cried about it. But we had also made the decision to put everything we had into the market, and we knew the risks. We might have felt defeated by that event, but we didn't. One thing saved us: we had confidence.

If you had asked me ten years before if I had confidence in my potential to be financially successful, the answer would have been a sad but certain no. And yet, there I was with a wife, a child, and a considerable chunk of savings ... that was now gone. But we had amassed those savings through a system I created, and I knew that despite the setback, we could do it all again.

Every Dime, Every Day. That's my system. It works not just because it's a step-by-step system that anyone can follow, but also because it builds confidence. You see, you never know what changes will come your way or what setbacks you'll have to face in the future, but you can know of your own abilities. This book represents a process that will give you the ability to start over, build again, and rise like a phoenix from the ashes because, as the Greek philosopher Heraclitus once said, the only thing constant about life is change. The question is, are you brave enough to make the changes you know you need to make?

THE TRUTH ABOUT CHANGE

Achieving financial freedom can't be something you kind of want to do or something someone else wants you to do. Just like with any profound change, such as losing weight or starting your dream job or business, the voice inside you that says it's time to take the leap has to be urgent. It has to be undeniable. And this voice has to be yours.

If you're reading this, and you aren't quite sure what your motivation is, or if it isn't strong enough, don't worry. I can help with that too. Skip ahead (this is the only time I'll tell you this!) to Chapter 3 and read "What Is Your Why?" and then come back here and start from the beginning. Once you've got a solid idea of why you want to make the changes necessary to achieve financial freedom, then you'll have a far greater chance of success. Why? Because gimmicks just don't work.

To quote Henry Ford: "The short successes that can be gained in a brief time and without difficulty, are not worth much." You've no doubt heard of and seen countless books and websites and blog posts about quick "tricks" and "tips" that will turn your whole financial life around. I get it. It would be really nice if you could give up a cup of coffee every week and magically have enough money to retire happily. Sadly, that's just not how it works.

9

Think about it. How many people do you know who have achieved lifelong health and wellness by following the fad grapefruit diet or that plan where you drink lemonade with cayenne pepper in it? My guess is no one. You might know someone who lost a few pounds, but if I were a gambling man, I'd say that the same person either gained those pounds right back or they were on to the next fad diet a few months later. Or both.

Here's the thing about gimmicks: people like them because they sound simple. Easy. Convenient. But how many worthwhile things in life are simple, easy, or convenient? We all know that the most important things require hard work, intense effort, and usually more than one difficult moment. Setting yourself free from debt and establishing real wealth is no different.

I know this because I have been there—stressed, deep in debt, disheartened. Then I started taking small, strategic steps to overhaul my financial life and habits. Those steps added up to a shift in how I thought about not just money, but also myself and my potential. I started with tens of thousands in debt, and I wiped out every cent of what I owed. Then I started saving, and I turned those savings into investments. But it took more than skipping a cup of coffee. It took real change. And I'm here to show you exactly how I did it.

It's the knowledge you gain throughout your life that matters more than the material things, because if you have the knowledge, then no matter what changes happen in your life, you'll still have the ability to overcome again. *Every Dime, Every Day* is the process I followed to transform my financial habits and ultimately my future. This book will give you the knowledge to make the same transformation in your own life.

THE *EVERY DIME, EVERY DAY* PLAN

My wife and I didn't just save more than $27,000 in the early years of our marriage; we also paid off a pretty sizeable debt. We'll talk more about how I got in and out of all that debt later because that was a big part of my learning how very much I wanted to avoid debt in the future. But first, let's talk about how the plan works—how it worked for me, and how it can work for you.

Assess. Stop wherever you are and look around. Think about your life. Are you where you intended to be? Are you doing the work you wanted to do and enjoying it? Are you stressed about your finances? Stuck in a rut? To quote Vance Havener, a rut is nothing but a grave with both ends kicked out. You just spin and spin and get nowhere, and then your life is over and you wonder what just happened? Whether you do this assessment and discover that you're nowhere near where you'd like to be, or you find that you're happy with where you're headed, the *Every Dime, Every Day* plan can help. With a plan, you can change directions entirely, or you can make sure that you stay on the path you're on in spite of adversity, like my wife and I did on Sept. 11, 2001.

Recalculate. Here's where the real details come in. Once you know the direction you truly want to take in life, or the goals you want to be pursuing above and beyond just paying your bills, it's time to put together a plan that will help you finance your dreams.

Make a plan. If you want to change the direction of your life—or to take your success even further—you need to do two things: 1. Rid yourself of any debt that's holding you back, and 2. Start building your savings. Here is how you can do that.

The *Every Dime, Every Day* plan divides your income into three categories:

1. **70 percent of your income should go to cost-of-living expenses.** This is your mortgage or rent, transportation, utilities, groceries, etc.

2. **20 percent of your income should go to paying down debts.**

3. **10 percent of your income should go into savings.**

Start keeping a logbook of all your spending. This is *key* to the success of *Every Dime, Every Day*. It's also the most challenging part for many people, and understandably so. It's going to feel tedious at first. Stick with it. Like any worthwhile habit, establishing a logbook takes persistence. But this is also why *Every Dime, Every Day* will work—why it will help you make your life what you truly want it to be. It's not a shortcut. It's a sure thing.

Following this plan, Erika and I had saved that $27,314 during the first few years of our marriage. We hadn't just saved, however ... we had done it while paying off the debt that I brought with me into our relationship. That's right. Me. Today, I run a highly successful financial services firm that invests in a multitude of stock market investments; I'm the owner of a million-dollar real estate company, serve as a motivational speaker and business trainer, and am a qualifier for the Top Tier of the Million Dollar Round Table—an honor achieved by less than one-half of the top 1 percent of all financial advisors. I don't say this to be boastful; rather, the people who helped me with this book made me put that in here to show you how far I've come. Back in 1998, when I married my wife, I was just a young man learning how to pull myself up out of decades of bad money habits.

Working Hard but Never Getting Ahead

When my parents were young, they found themselves unmarried and expecting me. Getting married did nothing to improve their situation. I'll never know if it was the financial pressure of having to support a child that caused my biological father to beat my mother, or if it was something else, but regardless, I'm grateful that his attempts to get her to lose the baby—who would grow up to become me— were unsuccessful.

It was over the course of the next few years that my mom met the man who would become my real father. They married and had two more kids, and I never felt like anything other than my stepfather's son. In fact, I didn't even know that he wasn't my real father until I was well into elementary school.

My mom and dad worked hard. They each had more than one job, and like so many people, they had dreams of a better life for their kids. Despite the fact that they were never able to save much, they managed to achieve their dream, in part, by moving us to a better neighborhood, where they bought a three-bedroom, one-bath house. When five people share a 1,200 square-foot space, it's tight. I shared a bedroom with my younger brother, and let me tell you, the idea of one day having my own room was probably one of my earliest motivations to be a hard worker.

And I was. Following the example of my parents, I started working early, and I worked hard. A neighborhood girl had the local weekly paper route, and I took notice of how successful she seemed to be. It appeared that she always had money to spend on the things she wanted, and since that's what I wanted, I decided to see if I could get a paper route too.

I started out with a smaller Wednesday route when I was eight, then added another route, and eventually got the weekly route, which was the toughest, being the biggest. All along I knew that reliability was crucial to my success, and that meant never missing a route, regardless of the weather, which, in Maine can be formidable in the winter! There were more than a few days when I'd be dragging a sled piled with papers up the street, knee-deep in snow. I got up at 3:30 or 4 in the morning to sort the papers, and eventually my routes got so big that I needed a central storage spot for the papers that I could return to and reload for each street. I ran into wild animals—skunks and moose—and on the rare occasion I was sick, my stepdad did my route for me.

There's that family work ethic. We had it. We, as kids, learned it and lived it. But what did I do with my money? I spent it.

Now, I'm not saying that you shouldn't spend any of your hard-earned money. But I am saying that you shouldn't spend *all* of it. You should save, and saving is a discipline you have to learn. I just didn't happen to learn it as a kid. I learned to work hard, and then I spent my money.

My parents only had so much to budget for things like clothes or sneakers, so if I wanted a nicer version of whatever they could afford, I would pitch in. I also spent my money hanging out with my friends in the neighborhood, and eventually I got a dirt bike that needed gas.

I mention all of this because it's the beginning of a pattern of spending, one that would haunt me for many years until I simply couldn't take it anymore. I blew every cent I made as young man. That's why when my son, who is now 18, got his first part-time job, we took him to the bank immediately to open two accounts: one checking and one savings. I knew it was my job to teach him the importance of always taking part of your check and saving it, putting it away someplace so that you can build something for your future.

WHO DO YOU THINK YOU ARE?

You have to give yourself permission to make your life better. Saving money is hard because you're investing in yourself—your future self. Sometimes it will be difficult for the people around you to support that decision, especially if they aren't investing in their future selves. In fact, it was just such a situation that lit a fire under me, a fire that has been burning ever since.

My Uncle Benny was part second dad, part big brother. As someone who was 10 years older, he was both my babysitter and friend. When his friends would play pickup baseball or basketball, Benny would always make sure I was included, even though I was a decade younger. As a kid, I idolized Benny.

On Friday and Saturday nights, Benny, my grandmother and some other relatives would sit around the table and play nickel or dime card games. One of those nights, when I was in my teens, I was going on about how I dreamed of stepping out and doing something different with my life. I remember there was a Molly Hatchet song playing—"Dreams I'll Never See"—and my Uncle Benny turned to me and said, "Listen to that song, Kevin. You're only a dreamer. Who are you to think you can do something different than the rest of us? You're no better than any of us."

It hurt, at the time, but ultimately it helped my self-confidence. We all have times when doubts creep in, when things aren't going as well as we had hoped, and we start to wonder: *Were all those negative people right about me? Maybe I'm not good enough to do any of these things I've dreamed of doing.* But then, you remember the people who said you couldn't do it. For me, I think about that night with Uncle Benny, and my next thought is always this: *I am going to prove them wrong.*

Benny was right about one thing, though. I'm not better at all. This isn't about being better than anyone. I just believe that everyone *deserves* better—less stress, a happier life, a more promising future. And I've created a plan that can help you, me—anyone—achieve that.

MAKE IT HAPPEN

Too often, people go through life stuck in a rut. They're working just to pay the bills, or living a life that simply isn't fulfilling, and in many cases, they don't even know it. If you don't stand up and stick your head out, you won't even realize how stuck you are. Life goes by so quickly, and there's no reason to spend it feeling stressed or disappointed. Regardless of age, situation, or circumstances, you *do* have the ability to stand up, look around, and ask yourself where you are and where you want to be—and then start moving in that direction.

BEFORE MOVING ON TO
THE NEXT CHAPTER:

Assess. Where are you now and where would you like to be? Is anything missing? Are there things you would like to be doing or working toward that you're not?

Recalculate. Make a list of your goals. For each goal, list the steps that will be necessary to get there.

Motivate. Make a list of the people who believe in you, the ones who will support you, but also include the people who you know are skeptical. They will provide that "I'll show them" motivation when you need it most.

Keep moving ahead. Don't worry about the "how" part right now. We'll get to that. Just start making a roadmap of the life you want to have, and then move on to Chapter 2. Together, we'll get there.

Chapter 2:
LESSONS FROM JOHN

It's better to hang out with people better than you. Pick out associates whose behavior is better than yours and you'll drift in that direction.

~ Warren Buffett

Remember when I had just turned in my Jeep and sat, tears in my eyes, in the backseat of my parents' car? It turns out, that moment was important for two reasons. First, change is hard, and that moment was exactly what I needed in order to actually follow through with the changes I would need to make. Second, it left me wide open to any wisdom or guidance that might help me.

As the often-quoted proverb goes, "When the student is ready, the teacher will appear." I'm here to tell you, that's the truth, and I know that because not long after my lowest moment when I voluntarily turned in my Jeep for repossession, John Jameson appeared in my path.

John was a teacher and owned an insurance brokerage as well. In his spare time, John worked with disadvantaged kids, volunteered at various places, and in general led an exemplary life. He still does. But when I met him, it wasn't at a volunteer gig or a school. It was at a hotel where I was attending a seminar about how I could potentially increase my income. I was 21, broke, in debt, and hungry for any information or opportunity that would help me change my direction in life. John was one of the presenters that day.

Immediately, I could see the potential that insurance offered. I joined John's group, got my insurance license, and began to soak up every ounce of knowledge that John offered. Each morning, we met at a restaurant, where we would set goals and plan our strategy for the day as we ate breakfast. Those breakfasts, and my time in the insurance business, marked a major turning point in my life, but not because I started making a ton of money. In fact, I hardly made any money at all. Instead, I gained the thing that I needed far more than money, since without it, money wouldn't have done me any good. I gained a whole new perspective.

YOUR ATTITUDE IS ALL THE DIFFERENCE

You hear it all the time, in a million different quippy quotes, but I personally had never really understood or believed how my attitude affected my life until it began to change. That change began before I was even aware of making it, because I was surrounding myself with a whole different kind of crowd. I was spending my breakfast hour goal-setting with a group of insurance professionals who had positive attitudes about their prospects and unmatched work ethics. They actually expected to be successful. They set goals and made plans, believing that those plans would work out, knowing that they could follow through.

Now, as I mentioned, I never made much money selling insurance. At the time, insurance sales were a door-to-door enterprise, and you needed reliable transportation and money for gas, neither of which I had. But what I lacked in practical resources I made up for in eagerness. I watched these people who were all moving in the direction of success that they had set for themselves, and I began to emulate them.

One of the things they did that I had never done before, or even considered doing, was *study how other people shape their lives.* It had simply never occurred to me that I could look at people whose lives I admired, learn how they made their lives successful, and follow their examples. Even more surprising to me was this: there were patterns. As I attended seminars and read more, I began to realize that all of these successful people had certain things in common. There was no secret, no magic password. Success was a learned behavior, and I simply hadn't been exposed to the right lessons yet.

LESSONS FROM JOHN

John recommended countless books, took me to seminars, and exposed me to all kinds of new ideas that truly changed my life. I would encourage every reader to seek out their own mentors, books, and influential experiences. Most of the worthwhile things in life are hard, and change is definitely one of them. In order to be persistent in the face of all that hard change, you need fuel. **Inspiration is the best kind of fuel for change.**

Here are a few of the things I learned from John in those early days that fueled my fire for change and kept it burning even when things got tough.

Believe. You have to change your beliefs about what you think you can achieve before real success becomes possible. This can be tricky because changing your beliefs often requires a change in actions. You have to believe that you can be successful in order to put in the hard work that success requires, but you won't do the hard work if you don't believe success is possible in the first place. This creates a seeming catch-22. If you *do* believe in your abilities, then the right actions will follow naturally, but if you're in a really low place and not feeling too sure of yourself, then you might need a little jumpstart. This is where taking action can be helpful.

Act. Action is a powerful catalyst. It's been said that you can't expect to achieve different results by doing the same thing; you have to do something different. The trick, then, is to start taking action, even if you're in that low place, even if at first you don't believe the actions will make any difference. Just doing something different from what you've done in the past has the ability to improve your attitude toward your prospects. Take action, and you'll see results, which will lead to a new belief in yourself, and inspire more action and more results. And here's a tip: one of the first actions you can take is to spend time with other people who are successful. Go hear someone you admire speak, attend a conference or seminar, take a class. Seeing other people succeed will help you believe that you can do it too.

Repeat. A habit is a recurring, often unconscious pattern of behavior that is acquired through frequent repetition. These are things we do every day, all day long, and as a result, they have a much bigger effect on our lives than we realize. To achieve freedom from debt, one of the first habits you'll want to consciously create is the keeping of a logbook. This is such a big deal, I've devoted an entire section to the subject in Chapter 4. When you feel like you have no idea where your money is going, how can you believe you'll ever have enough control to save any money, let alone amass any kind of wealth? But just start keeping the logbook, and very soon you *will* know where your money is going. What's more, you'll have the power to change where it's going, and make it go where you *want* it to go. Then you'll be saving, and as you watch that balance in your savings go up, something magical will happen. One day you'll realize that it's happened: you believe.

Belief, action, and habits are all interconnected. One tends to lead to the others. Believing in yourself equals confidence, and with confidence, your actions change, your habits change, and your expectations change. And when you expect positive outcomes from your efforts, suddenly those efforts are no longer so hard to put forth, and change becomes easier and easier.

Resist. Change isn't just hard for you. It's going to be hard for the people around you too. It's a sad truth, but there will probably be a few cases where people in your life, people who love you, will try to discourage you from changing, even if you're changing for the better. There are a lot of reasons for this, and you might never know exactly why it happens. In my case, my family hadn't experienced a lot of success, and when I had the audacity to imagine that I might make something more of my life, it was threatening to them. They felt that just by wanting more, I considered myself better than them somehow.

It's sad, but true: you're probably going to have to resist the discouragement of a few people who want to keep you right where you are. They don't believe that they can change their lives, and they don't want you to change either. Maybe they're scared. Maybe they genuinely think they're protecting you. It doesn't matter. You have to resist their negativity, rise above it, and carry on.

Rethink. Motivational speaker Jim Rohn is famous for saying, "You are the average of the five people you spend the most time with." As you begin the process of changing your life and moving toward a whole new level of success, it's worthwhile to rethink how you spend your time, and who you spend it with. Are you surrounding yourself with people who are equally invested in creating success for themselves? Whatever you want your life to be like, you should do your best to surround yourself with it. Just think: if your life is filled with negative people who don't believe that they can improve their situation, what are your chances of changing your own beliefs, behaviors, and outcomes?

HOW TO APPLY JOHN'S LESSONS TO CHANGE YOUR LIFE

Change your beliefs. Start by changing the way you think. Make it more positive. If you can't think your way to feeling better, then start taking action. Do things you've never done and go places you've never gone, even if at first you don't believe it will help. Look for opportunities to make your life better.

Change your expectations. Once you're looking at the world through a more optimistic set of eyes, you will start to expect good things of yourself, others, and life in general.

Change your habits. Take your new positive outlook and expectations, and change your habits accordingly. If you expect to live a healthy, active life, add a habit to match: start walking for 20 minutes every day, or skip the sweet snack you usually have in the evening. Act, believe, and repeat. Little habit changes bring big life changes.

Change your actions. Once you get an inkling of what you're capable of, you won't want to hold yourself back. A 20-minute walk will become training for a 5K. Saving $5 every day instead of buying a coffee every morning will become achieving your goal of being debt-free. Putting $500 a month into your IRA will become your retirement.

Enjoy the results. A positive change in one area naturally leads to positive actions and changes all over the place. Less financial stress, for example, will give you more energy for exercise or playing with your kids. Keep the positive beliefs, expectations, habits, and actions going and the positive changes will keep happening.

ARE YOU READY?

When I was truly ready, my mentor John appeared. He exposed me to a whole new group of people—people who believed in their potential to be successful. He introduced me to speakers and books and ideas that jump-started the change I wanted to make in my life. Now it's my turn. With this book, my goal is to teach you a structure for your financial life that, if you follow it, will ensure your continued success. But beyond that (and really, before that can happen) I hope to show you where you can find the fuel to inspire whatever changes you want to make in your life.

That fuel can come in many different forms. It might be lectures or classes, books, or videos. For example, if your ultimate dream is to leave your current job so that you can pursue the work you've always wanted to do, then maybe the inspiration that will fuel you best is seeking out a mentor in your chosen field. The key is to seek out whatever it is you need in the form of people and activities, so you can mentally prepare yourself for the success that is to come.

BEFORE MOVING ON TO THE NEXT CHAPTER:

Assess where you are.

Who do you spend the most time with? Do those people share the same motivation as you? Are they contributing to your success or taking away from it? Remember, you're the average of the five people you spend the most time with, so look around: do your closest companions reflect the life you want for yourself?

How do you think about money? Be honest. Does the thought of money fill you with energy or dread? Do you believe that you can shape your financial situation, or is your financial situation shaping you?

What beliefs and/or people are getting in the way of where you want to be?

Start seeking inspiration.

This book, I hope, will serve as a source of inspiration to fuel your life change, but also to start seeking other people, books, and experiences that will keep you going on your journey.

In this Internet age, inspiration is easier than ever to find. Start with the suggestions offered in this chapter, but also explore additional options for yourself. There is an almost limitless universe of webinars, podcasts, blogs, etc. out there, and you can never have too much inspiration!

Chapter 3:
SETTING YOUR GOALS

Our greatest weakness lies in giving up.
The most certain way to succeed is always to try
just one more time.

~ Thomas Edison

Though I didn't know it at the time, the years I spent working in the insurance industry would become the foundation for my life's work. At the age of 21, this wasn't my forever calling, but I will be forever grateful for the time I spent doing it. It exposed me to a whole new world of possibilities and positive thinking, and it prepared me for the next step, which was to get myself out of debt and devise a way to build some wealth. That was how *Every Dime, Every Day* (EDED) was born.

I've mentioned this before, but it bears repeating: change is hard. You need to be ready. You need to want it, to really and truly be prepared to give up some things that are comfortable and easy in favor of the things you really want, which are challenging but make your life worthwhile. Are you ready?

Before you start setting those goals, before you start tracking your expenses and making your life what you truly want it to be, you first need to identify your "why." This might seem like a no-brainer, but don't skip this step. It's what you'll come back to on the days when life gets real and change gets hard.

WHAT IS YOUR WHY?

Why ... it is the most important thing. In fact, it could be—and it is—the subject of entire books all on its own. If you want to make any kind of big change, it comes down to having a big enough reason. You need a lot of discipline to do the hard work that's required to reach any worthwhile goal, and in order to maintain that discipline, *you've got to have the why*. My why when I was starting out with the logbook was that I wanted to feel successful, to be successful, to make a better life for myself. I didn't want to feel like a failure anymore, and my feelings of failure were rooted in my inability to manage my money.

"A man in debt is so far a slave," as Ralph Waldo Emerson put it. I felt that slavery, and I wanted out. I wanted to be free. That was my why, and it was plenty to fuel any amount of discipline I would need to have. In fact, it still fuels me.

So what is your why? When you decided to buy this book, what prompted you to do so? What is motivating you to make this change and get your financial life under control? Before moving on to the next steps, you must figure out your why. It will make all the difference.

Here's an example: remember how Erika and I had just made our first big investment on Sept. 10, 2001? Well, I became licensed as a financial advisor in 2008, just when the economy took its famous mortgage crisis plunge. (Once again I had great timing, right?) I could have been blown out of the business. Many people were. It was a tough time for everyone in the industry, not to mention their clients. But I had created *Every Dime, Every Day*, a financial plan that changed my entire life and fortune, and I was determined to help people.

My why had been to get out of debt and save, but my new why consisted of two things: 1. To never go back to where I came from, and 2. To help other people change their own financial futures for the better. Notice that my why contained something I didn't want, and something that I did want. You can also frame your why using this structure. What experience was so awful, you never want to go back to it again? Who has the life that you want? What do you admire about their life? What kinds of things are they doing? How can you frame your why in terms of what you DO want?

As you think about your why, consider this: it has to be big enough. If your why is just, "I'd like to buy a fast car" or "I like designer clothes," that is probably not going to be enough. The work of gaining control over your finances is going to require real discipline, and your why for maintaining that discipline has to be rooted very deeply.

When I was first starting out, I faced a lot of criticism. Some of the people in my life told me I couldn't do this, that I wasn't good enough. If you can't find your why, think about that. Is there anyone who thinks you could never have enough discipline and control to make yourself wealthy? Are there people who don't think you're good enough for success?

Let's prove them wrong together.

SETTING YOUR GOALS

Once you know why you want to make this change, the next step is to figure out exactly what you want to accomplish—your goals. Just like your why, it's best if you can make your goals as specific as possible. Also, you need to make a few different kinds of goals: long-term, mid-term, and short-term. This will help you dream big but stay on track.

When I first started EDED, my long-term goal was to be debt-free. My mid-term goal was to eliminate all of my credit card debt first and my car loan debt second. For my short-term goals, I laser-focused on wiping out my credit card balances from smallest to largest. I could have just told myself, "I want to get out of debt," and then started putting any extra money I had toward my credit cards with no plan. But there are a few big problems with that:

Proof of progress. Without setting long-, mid-, and short-term goals, I would have had no way to track my progress. By setting short-term goals, I could see the steps along the way to my bigger, longer-term goals and know that I was staying on track.

Motivation. Without my short-term goals, my motivation might have lagged. See, every time I knocked out a debt, I felt such a rush of accomplishment. With each of your accomplishments, you will become more confident and more motivated. The whole process becomes easier and easier with every short-term or mid-term goal that you reach. And when you land squarely at that first long-term goal, it will blow your mind.

Erika and I used to dream about hitting the $100,000 mark one day. This is because at the time FDIC insurance, which protects you against the loss of your deposits in the case of bank failure (think Great Depression), covered each depositor for up to $100,000. I assumed that one day, when we reached $100,000, the bank would call us and say, "You should really do something about this money you've deposited because you're beyond the FDIC-insured $100,000 amount." I was thrilled at the idea of getting that call. The bad news is, that day arrived and no one called! No one emailed! Nothing. The good news is, that day DID arrive. For us, at the time, reaching $100,000 was really more of a dream than a long-term goal, to be honest. You never know what is possible until you go ahead and do it. And I am here to tell you, that's exactly what you can do.

WRITE IT DOWN

The key to achieving your dreams is simple: don't just set goals. Write them down.

I've been a financial professional now for many years, and a few things have become undeniably clear in that time. One of them is that people who write things down, who keep a physical record of their goals and progress, those are the people who achieve drastically greater success in achieving their goals.

One such couple comes to mind. We'll call them Ellen and Bob. Ellen and Bob came to me a few years ago to start preparing their retirement plan. Bob worked a manufacturing job much like the ones that employ many people in our area. Ellen was a homemaker and mother for a number of years, and then worked part-time at a local elementary school. You might expect that these two, even if they had done a decent job of saving, would have only low to average savings.

But the first thing that Bob and Ellen did when they sat down in my office was pull out the printouts of their spreadsheets: all of the income, all of their expenses, all for their entire married life. As you might guess, my eyes lit right up.

Ellen and Bob were millionaires. Like a lot of millionaires in America, you wouldn't know they were in that club by the lifestyle they lived. Like so many of the people I'm lucky to work with, they had amassed that wealth by following these rules:

- Live within your means.

- Spend less than you make.

- Be frugal savers.

- Have goals and a game plan to get there.

Ellen and Bob set goals for themselves when they first married, and they had decided to track everything to see how they were doing on those goals. And oh, how they did! They had jobs that weren't high-paying, but Ellen and Bob had managed to save more than three times what most people making the same amount are able to save. Because of the goals they had set, and the habit they had developed of recording everything they earned and spent, they were able to consistently live within their means.

You'll hear that a lot: *live within your means*. And it's true. Over 30, 40, or 50 years of saving, there will be drastic differences in the account values of people with jobs of similar wages but different money management styles. That's because, if you don't know where your money is going, what is coming in and what is going out, you can't live within your means. *You have no idea what those means are.*

HOW TO SET YOUR GOALS

As discussed earlier, you want to set three kinds of goals:

Long-term goals. These are goals that can be achieved within five years. These goals can change, just as any goal can, but they are more likely to shift because lots of things in your life can evolve within five years. If the goal does change, simply write a revised version and carry on.

Mid-term goals. These goals can be achieved within two years. In some cases, these might be goals that help you get to your long-term goals, like how paying off my credit cards was a mid-term goal that got me to the long-term goal of being debt-free. But sometimes these might be goals unto themselves. Maybe you want to save enough to buy a new-to-you (Buy used! See Chapter 12: Financial Common Sense) car. That's a goal that can be pretty easily achieved in two years if you're already carrying minimal debt.

Short-term goals. These are the goals you can accomplish within the next 12 months. Short-term goals work like benchmarks on the way to your mid-term and long-term goals. They allow you to stay on track and see your progress. As you cross off each one of your short-term goals, you will find a whole new level of motivation.

Strategies That Put Your Goals in Reach

Goals are your dreams in a concrete, achievable form. You want to be able to pay for your child's college? That's a goal. After decades of hard work, you want to spend your retirement finally seeing the world? That's a goal. But *how you make those goals a reality*, those are strategies. Fortunately, whatever your financial goals, the strategies that will make those goals possible are not terribly complicated. They require discipline and tenacity, but they are not complex. Those strategies, which we will discuss in detail in the next two chapters, are the logbook and the 10/20/70 rule.

There's another strategy, though, that you absolutely must implement if you want to be successful: *rewards.*

Even in our earliest days of implementing EDED, when my son was very young and my wife stayed home with him, we made sure to reward ourselves for all our hard work. Travel has always been one of our favorite things, and in those days, we went to Disneyworld. Every year, we would log all of our expenses and income, keep our expenses within our means, and save as much as possible. Then, when the time came, we would book our trip to central Florida and enjoy our reward. It was an inexpensive place to go, and it made our whole family happy. We never missed a trip, no matter how frugal we were trying to be, and some years we saved as much as 50 percent of our income.

These days, travel no longer has to be a reward. It's our way of life. We go on 10, maybe 12 trips a year. At some point, we got so into investing, that became one of our rewards instead. We'll set a goal, such as $25,000, and when we've saved that amount of money, we get to pick an investment.

WHAT IF YOU COULDN'T FAIL?

Before you move on in this book, I want you to think carefully about your goals. What is it that you're dreaming of? If you knew that you couldn't fail, what would you most want to do? What would your life look like? What would you do every day? Where would you live? How would your life be different than it is today? How would you feel about your life?

Take the time to answer these questions, and write your answers down. Next, start setting some goals that will help get you there. Remember to break them up into long-term, mid-term, and short-term categories. Don't set too many, because it's easy to lose focus—and besides, you can always set more goals once you knock a few out. Also, don't be afraid to dream too big. Maybe you have your sights set on something bigger than the FDIC insured limit. I hope you do!

Choose your first goals carefully and make sure you know your why. In the first months of establishing the EDED habit, sticking with the logbook can be a challenge. Saving and entering your receipts can be frustrating. At some point, you'll probably forget something or lose a receipt and want to give it all up. But if your why is strong enough, if your goals are clear and you have a well-defined plan, you will succeed. You will prove to yourself that whatever you dream, you really can make possible.

Be patient, and keep going. As you're reaching and achieving goals, your belief in yourself and in the process will also increase, and so will your vision of the next goal. **Success is the progressive realization of your worthwhile goals**. The key word, though, is progressive. The long-term goals will come, but only if you reach the short-term ones, reinforce your belief, and continue to move forward.

Before Moving on to the Next Chapter:

Figure out *why* you want to implement EDED in your life. You can have more than one reason, and that's just fine. Write all your reasons down so you can go back and look at them if the going gets tough.

Set at least one long-term goal, one mid-term goal, and three short-term goals that will act as benchmarks to keep you on track.

Remember, choose goals that are the most motivating and meaningful to you, and keep your goals to a minimum for now. You don't want to lose focus or get overwhelmed by having too many goals, and you can always set new goals when you've conquered your first ones.

Chapter 4:

THE LOGBOOK

If we keep doing what we're doing, we're going to keep getting what we're getting.

~ Steven R. Covey, *First Things First*

Were all looking for shortcuts. Just take a look at the magazine covers that surround you the next time you're waiting to check out at the grocery store: "Seven Ways to Slim Down Without Exercising," "Sleep Better with This Six-Second Trick," "Fix Your Finances in Five Minutes." There's really only one thing you need to know about all of these shortcuts: if they worked, there wouldn't be new ones on every magazine each week.

Shortcuts don't work. Or at least they don't work in the long term. If you want to make a real change in your life, you have to make a real change in your behavior. If you want to be healthier, you can't simply add an apple a day, and if you want to have healthier finances, you can't just save your change or stop buying coffee at Starbucks.

With your diet, if you want to make serious changes to your weight, you need to know how many calories you are taking in and how many you are burning. If you've ever attempted any kind of weight loss, you probably know that keeping a food diary (if you're totally honest) can be shocking. When people eyeball their serving sizes and guess their caloric intake, they notoriously underestimate how much they're eating. But when they make an honest and candid effort to weigh their food and record their actual intake, people tend to discover that they're eating far more than they thought they were, *and* they tend to lose weight.

People also don't tend to love keeping food diaries.

It's the same with your money. If you've never kept a log of all of the money you have coming in and all of the money you're spending, this will be a challenging habit to establish. But, just like that food diary, *it can also change everything for you.* It will be well worth the effort. The rewards are far beyond what you might imagine.

THE LOGBOOK HABIT

I started keeping my own logbook after hearing that financial speaker talk about his own little notebook. This was around the same time my mentor John suggested I take in some financial seminars. One of the speakers that stuck with me was a man who had created a tremendous amount of wealth. He talked about his own habits, one of which was a notebook where he wrote down everything he spent, every day. I immediately saw the value in that habit and began keeping my own logbook. Instead of a spiral notebook, I simply kept my receipts and wrote everything down in a logbook at the end of the day. It just seemed easier to me, but the spiral notebook idea was the beginning.

I started seeing places where I could spend less. I used to stop at the convenience store a lot on my way to and from work, or while running errands, and I would buy snacks and sodas. These seemed like tiny expenditures, and I honestly never gave them a thought until my logbook revealed to me that these mindless pit stops were costing me $50 or $60 each week. That was $200 or $300 each month that I could easily, painlessly divert over to paying off debt, and that's just one small example.

Using the logbook and the 10/20/70 rule (which we'll cover in Chapter 7 (titled: 10/20/70 Rule), I had already eliminated all of my credit card debt by the time another big change happened in my life.

A friend of mine introduced me to Erika, who was living in Manhattan at the time, working as a nanny. We talked on the phone at first, then agreed to meet for a date. After that, it was pretty much a done deal. In less than a year we were engaged and married.

One of the biggest challenges you can face when trying to implement EDED is a partner who isn't as committed to changing your financial habits and life. I was lucky. You might say it was meant to be because when I met Erika, she was already using her own form of a logbook. Her father had used a similar method of tracking his finances, and Erika had followed suit, a habit that allowed her to save $20,000 even while living in one of the most expensive cities in the world.

We were a great match, financially and otherwise, but it's not always the case that you and your partner will have the same financial habits and goals. If you are going to implement EDED successfully, though, you are going to need to work together and have a plan.

THE LOGBOOK PROCESS WORKS LIKE THIS:

Set up your logbook based on your expenses.

Save your receipts. Everyone who is spending money in the household (you, if you're single, or both partners) must save every receipt for every purchase.

Enter your receipts into the logbook at the end of each day.

At the end of the month, add up your expenses in each category.

If you are like most people, you'll want to focus on getting the logbook practice down for a few months before moving on to the next step, which is establishing a budget based on your expenses, income, and the 10/20/70 rule.

Be patient. Remember, this isn't a shortcut. Committing to save receipts for every cent that you spend and recording those expenditures and your income into the logbook is an every-day, all-the-time life change. That means you shouldn't expect it to take five minutes, five days, or even five weeks. You should commit to EDED and the logbook, and you should be patient with yourself if you don't get it perfect right away.

It took me three months before I finally got the logbook down perfectly and felt like it was truly a habit. In those early weeks, I would walk out of a store, toss my receipt in the trash, and not think about it again until that night, when I would sit down with the logbook and discover that I had messed up again. You might sit straight up in bed one night, realizing that you've totally forgotten to record your receipts for the day. It's going to happen. Don't worry about it. If you forget something, go back and fix it if you can, and if you can't fix it, forget about it and move forward. Above all, don't give up. In the words of Winston Churchill, "Success is not final, failure is not fatal: it is the courage to continue that counts."

WHY THE LOGBOOK?

We've already covered the practical reason for the logbook: because just like counting calories, we tend to underestimate and forget what we're spending unless we force ourselves to write it down. There's simply no good way to gain control of your spending, to figure out where your money is going, until you *buckle down and write it down.*

But, once I had mastered the logbook habit myself, I discovered a whole new reason for committing to the chore of the logbook (and yes, even for me it felt like a chore at first). The logbook helped changed my beliefs about money.

Remember in Chapter 2, how we discussed that in order to change your life, you first have to change your beliefs? Well, just deciding to change your beliefs is a hard thing to do. Maybe impossible. But sometimes you can change your actions, which can lead to new circumstances, and after a while, you start to see things differently. A new belief can form, and you'll gain a new perspective. For example, you might believe you absolutely need to own that second car. But then, if you start walking to work or taking the commuter train, you might realize that not driving to work lowers your stress level, and you can use the time more productively, and you can save more money than you thought possible, and—voilà!—your belief changes because you realize that, for now, you really don't need that second car. If you want to have a new perspective, you have to get up and move. That's what the logbook did for me.

Before I started keeping the logbook, I believed that I would never be successful financially. I believed that I would always be in debt, because I simply didn't make enough money, and so I would never have any money left over to save. Once I started writing down all of my income and expenditures, though, I started to see that there were ways to cut my spending, to find little bits that I could save. I also saw that, once I had cut out those expenditures, I didn't even miss them. Soon I saw that I was able to cut my spending enough to pay my way out of debt, and then those shavings were able to become actual savings. Every belief I had about money was totally turned on its head, *simply because I had started writing things down.*

SETTING UP YOUR LOGBOOK

Your logbook can be paper or digital, whatever you prefer. Choose something that is easy and comfortable for you. For example, a lot of people love Microsoft Excel for their budgeting, but for others, just thinking about using Excel is enough to bring on a migraine. If that's you, paper and pencil might be your best bet.

Erika and I have always used an accounting ledger for our logbook. Over almost two decades and a transformed financial situation, our little paper-and-pencil logbook has worked just fine for us. But you could also use an electronic spreadsheet or even a budgeting app. Regardless of the format you choose, the logbook setup is essentially the same.

Set up a page for each of your four main financial groups: **Income, Savings, Debts, and Expenses**. Expenses will probably require more than one page. Hopefully Debts will not! If it does, though, don't worry. You're on your way to wiping those debt balances out.

Now set up categories for each of those groups.

Income: If you have a regular job, this will simply be your paycheck. If you are self-employed, you will enter all of your income here. You should also include any other income in this category, such as money earned from rental properties, investments, etc.

Savings: This group will probably not have categories at first, but eventually, you might put your savings into several different kinds of accounts, such as regular savings, college savings accounts, retirement accounts, etc.

Debts: This is your Debt Knockout page, where each debt is listed with its balance and interest rate from largest to smallest.

Expenses: Because this category involves so many different bills and expenditures, it can be helpful to divide it into subcategories. Everyone will have their own unique setup, but here's an example to get you started:

- Category: House expenses

  - Subcategory: Rent/mortgage

  - Subcategory: Homeowner's insurance

  - Subcategory: Home maintenance supplies (toilet paper, cleaning supplies, etc.)

- Subcategory: Home maintenance costs (exterminator, lawn maintenance, etc.)

- Subcategory: Home security

- Category: Utilities

  - Subcategory: Electric

  - Subcategory: Gas/propane

  - Subcategory: Water/sewer

  - Category: Communications

  - Subcategory: Cell phones/landline

  - Subcategory: Internet

  - Subcategory: Cable

- Category: Healthcare

  - Subcategory: Health insurance

  - Subcategory: Prescriptions

- Category: Personal care

  - Subcategory: Salon

  - Subcategory: Massage, nails, etc.

- Category: Transportation

  - Subcategory: Gas

  - Subcategory: Car maintenance

  - Subcategory: Toll costs

- Category: Groceries

- Category: Entertainment

  - Subcategory: Eating out

  - Subcategory: Convenience store purchases (anything above and beyond groceries)

- Category: Travel

- Category: Taxes (for self-employed people, this would be your quarterly tax payments. Back tax payments would go under Debts.)

- Category: Donations

- Category: Childcare

- Category: Pets

  - Subcategory: Food

  - Subcategory: Vet bills

Once you have your logbook set up, you are ready to start recording your expenses. The process is simple:

Every time you spend any money, get a receipt.

Keep all of your receipts. You might consider keeping an envelope in your bag, purse, or car where you can collect receipts throughout the day.

Every evening, record your receipts.

MAKING THE LOGBOOK WORK FOR YOU

Remember to be patient with yourself as you set this up. There might be categories for things you don't realize you need until an expense comes up. Or you might need to adjust a category to make it broader so that it includes multiple things—for example, gifting to your church or charity, birthday presents, and holidays. First, just focus on getting the habit down. Collect your receipts, record your receipts. Adjust your categories as needed, and let the logbook reveal itself to you.

There will be some expenses that don't occur every month that you need to plan for. Car insurance, for example, is sometimes paid every six months. If it's too tricky to divide this up over each month, I simply put the entire expenditure in on the month I pay it.

Once a month, you will add up all of the categories in each group. This will help you create a realistic budget that follows the 10/20/70 rule. To stay on track, keep your expenses added so that you can ensure you're not overspending in each category.

Very soon, you'll start to see the changes happening. It might start small at first with an awareness of your spending patterns, and then a decision will be made to do something different. Your Savings will grow. Your Debts will shrink. And it's highly likely that your Expenses will shrink too. Just like when you commit to writing down everything you eat and drink, when you write down everything you spend, the practice alone causes you to think more carefully before you spend your money. Soon you'll find yourself spending less and cutting out unnecessary items. That money can be put toward paying down debt and paying up savings, and that's when the real results start to happen.

The first few months of getting this logbook habit down can be frustrating, but stick with it. Keep it up, and you will be surprised how quickly the results start to add up!

WHAT DO I DO WITH ALL THOSE RECEIPTS?

One thing the logbook habit will create is a GIANT pile of receipts. That might seem annoying at first, but trust me: it's a good thing. Each night after entering your receipts, put them into a manila envelope.

At the end of the month, seal that envelope up and put it in a file box. At the end of the year, you've got 12 manila envelopes in your box, each marked with its month and year, and you can seal up the box for the year and store it away.

Why would you do this? One reason: taxes.

No one ever wants to get audited, but it does happen. And if it happens to you, the logbook will be your best friend. Erika and I were audited a number of years back, and there was no panic. There was no stress. We simply took our boxes of receipts, organized in monthly envelopes, and our logbooks, and we walked right into the IRS office, where we were greeted by shocked expressions. I'd guess we were the only people who had ever come into an audit with every receipt organized and recorded. It's doubtful that anyone considers an audit fun, but that was definitely pretty close.

YOUR HOME IS A BUSINESS

Anyone who runs a successful business knows that you must always have a handle on your business expenses and income. You keep expenses as low as possible so that you can set your prices at an appropriate level to maintain competitiveness and the best possible profit margins. If that's what's required for a successful business, how could our household finances ever be successful if we have no idea what money is going out and coming in?

Treat your home like a business, and you are far more likely to be successful. The logbook is the first step to making that happen.

LOOKING BACK TO MOVE FORWARD

Another one of the great things about the logbook is that it gives you a physical, visual record of your progress. Since I've kept my logbooks going all the way back to 1998, I have this profound, incredible evidence of the journey I've taken. Sometimes I go back and look at those early logbooks just so that I can marvel at the progress I've made.

You're at the beginning of this journey, and I encourage you as you go along to keep everything. Not only is it simply a good business practice, but also—and more importantly—you are going to have such success that you might not believe how far you will go if you don't have a solid record of where you started.

Before Moving on to the Next Chapter:

Set up your logbook.

Start collecting receipts for all of your spending.

Record all of your receipts in the logbook each evening.

Record all of the income and money put into savings in your logbook.

Be patient! The logbook habit might take some time to get right. Even if you miss a receipt or forget an expense, keep going. Give yourself time to get it right before moving on. Remember, it took three months before I felt like I had the logbook habit down, so don't worry about getting it perfect right away. *The bottom line is not giving up.*

Chapter 5:

GOOD DEBT VS. BAD DEBT

*The only limit to our realization of tomorrow will be
our doubts of today.*

~ Franklin D. Roosevelt

M y mentor, John, didn't show up until I was ready to receive
the wisdom he had to offer, but even as a kid, there were
people in my life who offered a glimpse of what was
possible. My adoptive grandparents were one such beacon of hope.
Because they lived in Memphis, Tennessee, I only saw them once a year,
but I never forgot what it was like to visit their house. My grandfather
was the regional sales director for Gillette, and because they sponsored
the Miss America pageants, he often invited the current reigning Miss
America over to his house for dinner. Every time I visited their lives
seemed busy and exciting, and they always had plenty of everything
to share with their guests. I thought to myself, *Wow, look at what they
have created for themselves.*

Maybe you've also got a beacon of hope to look up to, a shining
example of what a good life might look like to you. Keep that in

mind to fortify your "why" as you tackle the subject of this chapter. As the quote above suggests, it's only your doubts that limit what your realizations of tomorrow might be. Doubt and the confidence-eating cancer that is debt.

I say this a lot, and I'll likely repeat it a few times in this book: bad debt is like cancer, and you need to fight it like a cancer patient fights for their life. If you allow debt into your life, it will eat away at every healthy, happy thing you have. I know this because I lived it, and that's also why I know that you can never create financial success without first addressing debt.

DEBT AND DESPAIR

In Chapter One, we talked about how hard work doesn't necessarily equal success. It won't matter how hard you work if you don't know how to handle your money, and a huge part of "handling your money" is avoiding debt. This is one skill that as a young man, I lacked. I knew how to work hard, yes, but I didn't know what to do with the money I earned, and furthermore, I had no idea how hard debt could go to work against me.

Remember the story of the boy, the Jeep, and a change for the better? Leaving behind my Jeep in that repo lot is one of my saddest memories, one that I will never forget. But I'm also grateful for that memory because in that moment, as I sat in the backseat of my parents' car crying, having failed so utterly despite my countless hours of hard work, I knew that I had to make a change. I couldn't live with that kind of despair, and I was ready to change, regardless of how hard it would be.

But first, how did I get there?

On the Road to Debt

I left Maine when I was 17 to go to Florida with my Aunt Joyce and Uncle Bob, who had an opportunity to open a new catering business. At that time, I thought maybe the restaurant business would be my future. I knew it inside and out, and, so far as I could tell as a very young man, I liked the work. Unfortunately—or, rather, fortunately, but I wouldn't know that for years—the new catering business didn't pan out. Instead, I enrolled in a high school there and finished my diploma while working 50 hours a week as a Burger King shift manager.

There it is again: hard work. But what was I doing with my earnings? I was spending them. What's worse, I was spending more than I made. I wasn't being extravagant, though. Not in my mind, anyway. My first new car was a 1989 Toyota Tercel, not a Corvette, and I waited until after I graduated and moved back to Maine before I bought the Jeep.

That purchase was inspired by the success of an exciting opportunity. I was hired by a local convenience/liquor store owner to add a food operation to their existing business model. Today, gas stations have all kinds of food options, but in those days, you bought gas at gas stations, along with maybe oil and possibly cigarettes. Food was not part of the equation. So, it was a new and exciting task for me to figure out the entire business model, from sourcing to profit margins. I created this operation from the ground up—a thrilling task for my young, hard-working self—and added a profitable revenue stream to the business. I was proud of that, and buying the Jeep felt like a hard-earned reward. I looked at what I earned, what I felt I could afford, and I bought myself a new car because, at the time, I didn't know what "afford" really meant.

Now, I know better. When it comes to a long-term, big-ticket item, affording something doesn't just mean that you can pay for it today or this month, or even this year. If you're signing on to be the owner of something with a big price tag, you'd better be able to handle that entire price tag every day *even if your circumstances change*. Because change they most certainly will. Mine sure did.

49

In addition to gas, the store also sold liquor, and as a result, it was the target of frequent shoplifting. Anytime I was on duty, it was also my job to look out for shoplifters. One evening, a shopper dropped several bottles into her bag and then left the store. I followed and stopped her, but instead of a simple confrontation, she attacked me.

That experience opened up a new awareness in me, and I started hearing about other gas station robberies. In the end, my safety won out over my financial security. I left that job and then had trouble finding another. That was when all my credit card spending caught up with me. It was also when the payments for my new Jeep became more than I could manage.

FINANCIAL CRISIS

If you've fallen into the habit of spending more than you earn, if money worries keep you up at night and debt feels like a noose around your neck, you're not alone. According to the Pew Charitable Trusts, one in three American families have no savings whatsoever, and of that third, one in 10 of those families make more than $100,000 per year.[1] That's particularly scary and stressful when you take into account the fact that 60 percent of American families experienced a financial shock—such as a sudden car repair or a cutback in work hours—in the last year.[2]

If that sounds like you, it's time to make a change. You don't have to wait until you're facing financial despair like I was that day in the backseat of my parents' car. You don't have to wait until that moment when you feel like all is lost, but I will tell you this: *you do have to be ready.* You have to have the desire, and you have to be committed.

---

1 http://www.pewtrusts.org/en/research-and-analysis/issue-briefs/2015/11/emergency-savings-what-resources-do-families-have-for-financial-emergencies

2 http://www.pewtrusts.org/en/research-and-analysis/issue-briefs/2015/10/the-role-of-emergency-savings-in-family-financial-security-how-do-families

It's not easy. But it is possible. I did it, and so can you.

Bad Debt vs. Good Debt

No matter how hard you work, if debt is siphoning away everything you earn, you will never get ahead. That's why, before we get into how to set up your new, successful financial plan, we first have to get eye-to-eye with the debt monster hiding under your financial bed.

Debt is a particularly difficult issue because all debt isn't created equal. Without a clear understanding of which financial decisions are hurting you and which ones are helping, it can be almost impossible to get a handle on your overall money situation. Let's take a look at some of the different kinds of debt.

The American Heritage Dictionary defines debt as "something owed, as in money, goods, or services." That's the simplest, easiest definition to understand: you owe money, and that is a debt. Many people would say that owing anything—any kind of debt at all—is bad. There is a good reason for that perception. You'll usually find that the lender—the person who has the money—benefits most from debt. There are, however, situations in which some debt, under specific terms and conditions, can be good.

What is a "good" debt? Well ... it depends. I'm a big proponent of learning, of taking knowledge and inspiration from experts, and one of my favorite financial experts is Robert T. Kiyosaki, author of the bestseller *Rich Dad, Poor Dad*, among other books. Kiyosaki draws a definite line between good debt and bad debt: bad debt, he says, makes you poorer, and good debt makes you richer.

How can a debt make you richer, though? Real estate is a good example. You could purchase a property using a small down payment of your own money and a mortgage. Then, if you rent that property out, your tenant is paying your mortgage, taking care of your debt, and building equity for you all the while. Technically your mortgage is debt, but in that case, the debt gives you the opportunity to increase your wealth.

I warn you, though: those "good debts" are much rarer than bad debts. Bad debts, such as credit cards, are everywhere. Plus, even good debts, such as the mortgage example we used above, can be risky. What if, for example, you invested in that real estate, but then you were not able to rent the property? Not such a good deal anymore.

ASSET VS. LIABILITY

This discussion of good and bad debt brings up another tricky issue—one that many people think they understand but don't. Let's take a look at assets versus liabilities.

An asset, like a good debt, helps you get richer, while a liability takes away from your wealth. Let's go back to that real estate example. If you buy a house with a mortgage and then rent it out, it's making money for you, right? That's an asset. But what about the house you live in? That's a bit trickier. The longer you own that house and pay your mortgage, the more equity you will have in your home and the more that asset will be worth. But if you own a $200,000 home with a $180,000 mortgage on it, that's not much of an asset, is it? What's even worse is that many people—3.2 million in 2016—owe more on their mortgages than their homes are actually worth.[3]

A TRUE AND HONEST INVENTORY

In Chapter 1, you spent some time considering what kind of life you would like to have. Before you can head out on that journey, though, you have to figure out where you're starting. Our goal in this chapter is to take a good hard look at where you're standing in terms of your debt. A small warning—this is one of the least fun parts

3 http://www.cnbc.com/2016/04/04/how-are-millions-still-underwater-as-home-prices-rise.html

of the whole *Every Dime, Every Day* process. Chances are pretty good that if you're reading this book or thinking about using EDED, your current financial picture isn't what you'd like it to be. But be brave. If you take a hard, honest look at your assets and liabilities right now, you will be able to start changing that picture, no matter how painful. If you're not honest now, those changes will be harder, maybe impossible to make later on. Why? Because sooner or later, the monster that is debt will crawl out from under the bed and catch up with you.

Before Moving on to the Next Chapter:

Create an assets and liabilities inventory. On a sheet of paper (or a document/spreadsheet on your computer), make two columns: "Assets" in one, "Liabilities" in the other. In the Assets column, list everything you own that has value, along with the actual value *right now*. For example, if you own a house and that house is appraised at $180,000, that's what you would list in the Assets column. If, however, you have a mortgage on that house for $130,000, you would list that in the Liabilities column.

Debt Consolidation

The average American household owes nearly $16,000 in credit card debt. Thanks to all that debt, advertisements for consolidation loans are everywhere. It certainly can be tempting to get a debt consolidation loan to pay off all of those credit cards and combine your debt into a single lower-interest loan, but there's a danger here. Consolidation loans can backfire in a number of ways. For one thing, a lot of the consolidation loans out there come with exorbitant interest rates and unfavorable terms. But even more importantly, most people use their consolidation loans the wrong way and end up racking up even more debt.

For example, let's say you're paying $1,500 each month on your credit cards just to make the minimum required payments. You get a consolidation loan and pay off those cards, which lowers your monthly payment to $1,000. What do you do with the extra $500 each month? Well, it's not *extra*. That money should go directly toward debt to pay down what you owe faster. Unfortunately, that's not usually how it's done. Consolidation loans make you feel like you have extra cash when you really don't. That's why it's better to skip consolidation loans altogether and go with the Debt Knockout, which we'll discuss in the next chapter.

Examples of assets: home, car, investments, savings and checking accounts, universal life insurance, anything of value.

Examples of liabilities: credit card debt, mortgage, taxes owed, car loan, personal loans, student loans.

Be honest. As you make your list, be clear and honest with yourself about the value of your assets. For example, you might have purchased an amazing, luxury sofa for $5,000, but the moment you took that sofa out of the showroom, it decreased in value. **Ask yourself how much you could sell that sofa for right now: that is the value of your asset.** The same goes for your car. No car is worth what you paid for it. Depreciation always takes its toll, and when you buy things new, depreciation will hit even harder. New cars lose 10 percent of their value the moment you drive off the lot, and they continue to lose 15-25 percent of their value each year for the first four years of ownership.[4]

---

4 https://www.nerdwallet.com/blog/credit-card-data/average-credit-card-debt-household/

https://www.carfax.com/guides/buying-used/what-to-consider/car-depreciation

Chapter 6:
THE DEBT KNOCKOUT

Wars in old times were made to get slaves. The modern implement of imposing slavery is debt.

~ Ezra Pound

If you've gotten to this chapter, a few things must be true:

- You're exhausted from financial stress.

- You're ready to make some strategic changes in your financial life.

- You've taken some time to rethink your life goals.

- You've created a list of your assets and liabilities.

So here we are. Take that list of assets and liabilities and lay it out in front of you. In this chapter, we're going to make a plan to deal with the liabilities section of your list, all of which are debts.

Keep in mind what we discussed in the last chapter: bad debts versus good debts. Many people will want to use the Debt Knockout to pay off their bad debts only, while keeping their good debts. When I first began devising the EDED program for myself, I focused on bad debt first—credit cards specifically.

By the time I met Erika, I had paid off all of my credit card debt and only had a $6,000 car loan left in terms of total debt. Using the $20,000 Erika had already saved, we paid off the car loan and started our marriage $14,000 to the positive. Now debt-free, Erika and I made the decision that we never wanted to be in any kind of debt again, either good or bad. We set a goal of saving enough to buy our first house without having to get a mortgage. You probably think that sounds impossible, but remember: that's the whole point of this book, that *all of this is possible*. If we can do it, so can you.

A house could be considered a bad debt: it doesn't put money in your pocket, so it is a liability. That was the right goal for us, but you have to decide what's best for you. If you're planning on living in a house while it appreciates, perhaps because of some work you do to it or a particularly strong market, then you might consider a mortgage a good debt. Regardless, things like credit cards and car loans are never good debts. That's what we're going to focus on eliminating first with the Debt Knockout.

Think back to your days at the carnival as a kid, those fair games you just couldn't stop playing until you won. That's how the Debt Knockout works too. It works if you treat it like a competitive game.

Why Debt Matters

Think of your financial plan as your own personal ark. It's pouring out there, but you have an ark, and it can ensure you and your family stay safe and dry. However … you've got debt and every debt is like a hole in the hull of your ship. No matter how well the ship is built, if there are holes in the bottom, you'll never stay afloat. So, our mission is to eliminate your debt first, and then we can build the most seaworthy, sound financial ark you could ever imagine. That's where the Debt Knockout comes in.

HOW DOES IT WORK?

The ball you're going to use to knock out your debts is this: 20 percent of your income (See Chapter 7: 10/20/70 Rule). Minimum payments would be like throwing a handful of pebbles at your debt. You're unlikely to knock very much down, and if you do, it will take a lot more effort and time. That's because the companies who own your debts charge interest, and when they tell you what that "minimum payment" will be, they're counting on you thinking that means it's an acceptable amount to pay. It's "acceptable" to them because it's how they make millions. But it's far worse for you. You might have a credit card that only requires you to pay a small percentage of your actual balance each month, which means:

It will take much longer to pay off your debt.

You will pay a tremendously larger amount overall before you finally do pay it off.

There is no reason to give your money away. Tell yourself that right now: *I will not give my money away.* And luckily, there's a way to pay off your debts without giving away money that you ought to be able to keep, and it's called the Debt Knockout.

HOW IT WORKS

The Debt Knockout helps you organize your debts so that you can pay them off strategically, making the most of the 20 percent of your budget you're dedicating to debt. It's like putting down that fist of pebbles, picking up a softball, and then chucking it at each debt one at a time. When you knock a debt down, you get an even bigger ball to throw at the next debt.

Like every step of EDED, the Debt Knockout isn't difficult to do. It does, however, require organization, follow-through, and, above all, tenacity. Follow the steps below and stick with the process, and you'll see results that are so motivating, you'll never slide back into debt again.

SETTING UP THE DEBT KNOCKOUT:

Write down all of your debts, starting with the largest balance and ending with the smallest.

Write the interest rate of each debt in a column next to the balance. For example, you might have $300 on one credit card with a 16.8 percent APR (Annual Percentage Rate), $5,200 on another credit card with a 12.5 percent APR, and a car loan of $10,000 with a 4.1 percent interest rate. You also have a mortgage of $150,000 with a 3.9 percent interest rate, but we're going to leave that off the Debt Knockout for now so that we can put our laser focus on the debt that is hurting you most. [Insert an image of an example Debt Knockout list.]

With your list created, every hole in your financial ship is right there in front of you. There's no hiding

DEBT IS TRICKY

The terms of any debt you owe are trickier than you might imagine. That's by design: if you're foggy on how disadvantageous the deal is for you, you're less likely to refuse to agree to them!

Your Annual Percentage Rate (APR) can be found on your credit card statement each month [insert an image of the section of a credit card statement where the interest appears]. Note that the terms "APR" and "interest rate" are used interchangeably, but your actual APR typically includes fees and can be higher than the stated interest rate that you think you're paying. Also, you might think you have a fixed interest rate, but there are a few APR tricks that your credit card company can pull on you, and you should be aware of them. Be sure to check for changes on your statements every month.

Late payments can make your interest go up. Somewhere in the very long, wordy credit card agreement that you were sent when you signed up is probably a clause that states the company will raise your APR (even if it's a 0 percent for X amount of time promotion) if you are late with a payment. You'll also be charged a late fee, which means that you're hit with an immediate penalty and a long-term, ongoing penalty for missing just one payment.

Actually, credit card companies can change your APR anytime. Credit card from it anymore, but hey, how can you fix a hole that you can't see? This is the only way to safeguard your financial future so that you can start moving ahead into the future of wealth that you deserve. Here's what happens next:

The goal is to knock out the smaller balances first. Let's say that you have $700 each month to put toward debt. Your Debt Knockout list looks like this:

companies often snag you with an enticingly low introductory APR, but that APR will end, and once it does, that company can and will raise your interest rate. When they do, they will notify you, but that notification could come at the bottom of a looooong email or as an easily missed line in a letter. It's up to you to stay on top of your APR changes. You can be sure your credit card company won't help.

$10,000	4.1%
$5,200	13%
$300	16.8%

Your minimum payments will change each month based on how much of the principal you've paid, your APR, fees, etc. In general, though, the idea is to pay the minimum payment on everything except the smallest payment. Let's say your minimum payments look like this:

$10,000	4.1%	Minimum payment: $240
$5,200	13%	Minimum payment: $108
$300	18%	Minimum payment: $15
Total minimum payments		$348

With a $700 debt payment budget, after paying $348 to your minimum payments, you've got $352 left ... and look! You can pay off that small debt right away. Strike that debt off your list completely. If that debt was a little larger, you would simply keep paying the largest amount (whatever's left after your minimum payments) to that smallest debt until you can strike it off.

When you knock a payment out, first you celebrate. Then you take the money you were using to pay that debt and roll it up to the next one.

Maybe you've heard the Albert Einstein quote, "Compound interest is the eighth wonder of the world. He who understands it, earns it ... he who doesn't ... pays it." Well, you have a choice: you can pay that compound interest on your credit cards and give away your money, or you can learn how to compound your payments and get out from under those debts faster and at far less expense in the end. That's money you get to keep so that it can work for you. More on that in the upcoming chapters. Get your Debt Knockout set up, and keep pushing forward!

Before Moving on
to the Next Chapter:

Make your Debt Knockout list.

You can begin your Debt Knockout strategy whenever you're ready. In the following chapters, you will be getting a better handle on where your money is going, and then you will be able to create a budget that follows the 10/20/70 rule, with 20 percent of your income going to pay off debts. For now, put as much money as you can manage toward your debts. There's no time like right now to start getting rid of the debt that's preventing you from enjoying the wealth you deserve!

Chapter 7:

10/20/70 RULE

*I found the road to wealth when I decided that a part
of all I earned was mine to keep. And so will you.*

~ George S. Clason, The Richest Man in Babylon

Always keep learning. If you do that, you will always be richer,
no matter what your bank account looks like. Not every idea
will be right for you or make sense to you, but if you can read
a book or attend a seminar and bring away one good idea that helps
you make your life better, then it was worth the time and money
you invested. That was something my mentor John taught me, and it
might sound strange, but that was a revelation to me as a young man.
School wasn't something I disliked, but it wasn't my favorite thing, or
something I particularly excelled at as a kid. So when, as an adult, I
rediscovered learning and what a difference it could make in my life,
I was pretty much shocked.

One of the first books my mentor John recommended to me, and
one of the books that I still return to over and over, is *The Richest Man
in Babylon* by George S. Clason. In that classic book about how to

achieve financial freedom, I first came across the idea that if you spend everything you make, you will always be a slave.

The key to becoming financially free is to change how you think of the money you earn. Most people treat their earnings like food: they earn it and consume it. Then it is gone. But the people who are financially free think of their money a bit differently. It's not food. It is SEEDS. Your earnings, if you keep them for yourself, can be used to grow more money. First, though, you have to figure out something that so many people never learn: how to keep a part of everything you earn. That's where the 10/20/70 rule comes in.

What Is the 10/20/70 Rule?

You begin with the logbook so that you can get a clear idea of how much money is coming in, how much is going out, and where all of that money is going. Once you've established the logbook habit, and you're aware of where your money is going, it's time to take control of your money. The 10/20/70 rule is the structure for a budget that will allow you to establish spending and saving patterns that will ensure you are keeping part of everything you earn. It works like this:

10 percent of your income goes to savings

20 percent of your income goes to paying off debts

70 percent of your income goes to lifestyle

10 Percent Savings

Let me be very clear: this 10 percent is a minimum. The more you can put toward savings, the better. This category of your budget should never be decreased, only increased. For example, let's say you pay down your debt to zero. You would have extra money that, theoretically, you could spend, but I would suggest that you put at least part of it toward savings.

20 Percent Debt

Saving is always important, but you will never be financially free until you eliminate debt. For that reason, 20 percent of your income should go to paying off debt. Remember the Debt Knockout we set up in Chapter 3? Well, get that sheet of paper out and refamiliarize yourself with it because that's where this 20 percent of your income is going to go. Until every last debt is paid off, you will be dedicating 20 percent of your income to this category.

This is also a category that should never decrease. As long as you have debt, you should be allocating a minimum of 20 percent of your income toward paying it off.

There are ways to help decrease the amount of debt you rack up each month with interest charges, and they are all strategies you should implement.

Get all three free credit reports—Experian, TransUnion, and Equifax—each year. There is no need to pay for these reports, so don't fall into any online traps.

Check each credit report for mistakes. Are there things on there that are incorrect? Are there reports that are lowering your credit that should have been removed? Aside from bankruptcy, negative items are only allowed to stay on your credit report for seven years. But that doesn't mean they actually come off in a timely manner. It's your responsibility to check your report to be sure that all of the data is correct and timely. And of course, you always want to be sure that everything on your credit report is actually yours: millions of people are victims of identity theft each year.

Call your credit card companies and ask for a lower interest rate. Be polite, be patient, and, if necessary, ask to speak to a manager. Credit card companies are motivated to keep customers, and in many cases, they will work with you to lower your interest rate, which can save you thousands of dollars over time.

Consider refinancing your mortgage carefully. People often refinance their mortgage to lower their monthly payments, but there are two problems with this. First, if you lower your payments, but then immediately spend that money rather than put it toward debt or savings, you've lost all of the benefit of your refinancing. Also, refinancing costs money: if you cannot lower your interest rate by at least a couple of percentage points, it is probably not worth the thousands you'll pay in fees to refinance.

70 PERCENT LIFESTYLE

When I began using the 10/20/70 rule myself, eliminating debt was my goal. I wanted not just to eliminate it, but also to eliminate that debt as quickly as possible, so instead of dedicating 20 percent of my income to paying off debt, I used 35 to 40 percent of my income. When I made that increase, however, I didn't take any money from savings. I continued to put 10 percent of my income to savings no matter what. Instead, I took a hard look at my lifestyle spending and cut out every extra thing I could.

What is lifestyle spending? This is everything you spend money on that isn't a debt. Lifestyle spending includes:

- Rent/Mortgage

- Utilities

- Groceries

- Entertainment

- Clothes

- Tuition

- Childcare

- Gas

- Insurance

You get the point. Everything except credit cards or loans (which are debt) would be considered lifestyle spending.

Some of these items, like entertainment and clothes, are things that you have a lot of control over. You can even eliminate some spending. Buying a $3 coffee every morning on the way to work is a great example. With 52 weeks in a year and five workdays a week, you'd be spending that $3 on 260 days, adding up to a shocking $780 spent on coffee. For a lot of people, that's a mortgage payment. Two car payments. That's a lot of money—a lot of money you could be using to pay down debts.

Other expenses, like rent and utilities, you can decrease somewhat by being responsible and living within your means, but you're unlikely to eliminate them (unless your parents are willing to let you live rent-free in their basement for a while!).

Your logbook will help you see all of your spending habits, and when you can *see* where your money goes, you can *change* where your money goes.

Once I had paid off all of my debt, I could have moved that money back into the lifestyle category. Instead, I had a new goal: Erika and I wanted to save enough money to buy our first house. Immediately, all of the money I had been spending to pay down debt went into savings. It seemed like a pie-in-the-sky sort of goal, being able to write a check for an entire house, but it turned out that wasn't true at all. By tracking all of our spending with the logbook and structuring that spending with the 10/20/70 rule, we were able to make that dream come true in a matter of just a few years.

You can too. You truly can.

Q&A Session

What if I can't make 70 percent of my income fund my lifestyle expenses? The answer to this is simple, but it isn't easy: you CAN. In many cases, when people think they could never live on 70 percent of their income, that's just a matter of not knowing where their money is going. That's why the logbook habit comes first. Once you see where you're spending your money, you will definitely find some expenditures that surprise you. People often spend on things that don't seem like much in the moment, but when taken all together, those little splurges add up quickly and surprisingly. When you're aware of them, you can cut them out, and you probably won't even miss them that much. You particularly won't miss them much if you remember two things:

Your goals and why they are so important to you.

Your reward.

How do I fit rewards into my 10/20/70 budget? Rewards should be a planned expense, and they should come out of the 70 percent of your lifestyle expenses. For my family, the reward, as I mentioned before, was Disneyworld. Some years we were saving as much as 40 or 50 percent of our income, but we never missed our trip to Disneyworld. We budgeted, and we looked forward to it. Just seeing the progress you are making at freeing yourself from debt and reaching your financial freedom goals will be motivating in itself, but having a reward that means a lot to you might just give you the extra motivation to skip the indulgences that throw your spending out of line.

ADJUSTING YOUR LIFESTYLE FOR A BETTER TOMORROW

It's not easy to give up things that you want, particularly if they are things you've been accustomed to giving yourself anytime you want them. Most of us are familiar with this. Maybe we've dieted and felt the pain of denying ourselves the small treats we once took for granted. Maybe we've had a baby, and those middle-of-the-night feedings taught us that giving up sleep can be rough. But then consider the rewards of those sacrifices. Wasn't it worth the skipped cookies or

French fries to feel healthier and stronger? And when you finish those months of all-night infant care, don't you enjoy and value a good night's sleep so much more than you ever did before?

The same goes for spending. You might think that you "need" the extra things you're buying now, but what if you waited just a bit? Would you still need them? And what if you found that you DID need them (or at least you wanted them a lot), but that you could save for them and still get them without going into debt or dipping into your savings?

The concept of delayed gratification isn't a very popular one these days. I would suggest, though, that it's worth another look. Not only are things more enjoyable when you have to wait for them, because you have the opportunity to anticipate how much you will enjoy them—a gratifying experience all by itself—but also you get the added (and even more important) benefit of knowing that by waiting and staying within your budget, you are building a future for yourself that is so much brighter.

Put simply, would you rather have that new TV today or be able to travel in your retirement? Or, even more critically, what if you needed a special treatment or doctor in your older years? Would you trade a new car now for being able to give yourself the best healthcare later in life? When you consider how dearly you pay in interest when you go into debt, the tradeoff might be exactly that dire.

One last thing: delayed gratification is a great skill to teach your kids. If you have children, chances are you already know that a kid who expects to get everything he or she wants the instant he or she wants it is pretty challenging to deal with. Delayed gratification is good for them now, and it's good for them in the future. If your kids can say no to the newest pair of shoes or technological toy, they will be far more likely to build up their savings and not go into debt. And isn't that something you want for them?

Always keep in mind (and if you have kids, remind them too): all of this delayed gratification is for a very worthwhile purpose—to ensure a happier, more secure future in which you can make your dreams come true.

YOU DESERVE TO BE IN THE DRIVER'S SEAT

We often feel that we "deserve" special treats, little (or not so little) expenditures for how hard we work. But that's only partly true. What's more important, and *what you really deserve* is to be in control of your financial life, to have the peace of mind that you will be able to take care of yourself and your family, and to know that you can make your own dreams come true. But financial control, saving, and delayed gratification—these are all learned skills. Not all of us learned them growing up. I know I sure didn't. With *Every Dime, Every Day*, you can change that.

The logbook, which you've been using for three months (or less, depending on how comfortable you were with tracking your spending before), helped you discover where your money is going, and now the 10/20/70 rule will help you create a budget that puts you in the driver's seat, so that you can send your money where you *want* it to go.

BEFORE MOVING ON
TO THE NEXT CHAPTER:

Create a budget that divides your income into the three 10/20/70 categories:

10 percent savings

20 percent debt

70 percent lifestyle

Continue using the logbook to track your income and spending to ensure you are staying within your budget.

Adjust your spending as needed.

Chapter 8:
FINDING THE RIGHT
FINANCIAL PROFESSIONAL

If you have more than $50,000 to invest, you should
fire your broker and find an investment advisor.

~ Arthur Levitt, Former SEC Chairman

As with any profession, not all financial professionals are created equal. There are brokers, planners, and investment advisors; some professionals work on commission while others are fee-based; some have certifications and a great range of skills, while still others are held to higher standards and have chosen the road of transparency. What do these different choices mean to you, the investor? How do you judge whether you've got a good one, or whether you are getting good service from one? How do you know what to look for, or even if you need one?

Making the choice to get debt-free, delay gratification, and put a savings plan into place is hard work. You want to know that your efforts will be rewarded in the best way possible, and if you have already done this hard work, then you want to know that your portfolio is being managed in the best way possible. This is where the guidance of a financial professional can literally help you earn thousands more in returns and save thousands more in fees, inefficiencies, and tax mistakes. Before we carry on with your EDED plan, it's time you start thinking about how to find the right financial professional to guide you as you build your new financial life.

DO I NEED TO HIRE SOMEONE?

The choice to work with a financial professional is a personal one, and many factors come into play when making this decision. The truth is, financial planning becomes more complicated the older you get because as you age, you generally accumulate more assets, more savings, and more responsibilities. Some people are motivated to seek the help of a financial professional because they have people in their lives they want to take care of, such as a disabled child or a spouse. Other people wait until an emergency situation occurs, such as the sudden death of a family member, and the situation becomes dire.

I personally experienced a situation during the editing process of this book that brings home this point. One evening during a weekend business convention, I was mugged while walking along the boardwalk in Atlantic City. When I regained consciousness, I was lying on a hospital gurney with the concerned faces of doctors and nurses hovering above me, and my first thought was my family. I thought about my wife and my son, and I had a sense of peace. At forty-six years old, I knew that if I didn't make it out of this scrape alive, I had at least done enough at this point in my life to take care of the people I loved. They wouldn't have to endure financial hardship, our son would be able to go to college, and my wife would be able to stay in our home.

Granted, financial planning is what I do for a living, but what I preach to my clients is what I put into practice for my own life. All of our paperwork is in place, our investments are being managed, beneficiary designations are up to date, and I designed a succession for my business. Even William Bengen, the financial professional responsible for coming up with the 4 percent rule, has hired not one, but *two* financial advisors to manage his assets during retirement.[5] These are not empty words. I want you to have the peace of mind that planning brings so that no matter what happens, your assets will grow in the most efficient manner possible, your belongings will be taken care of as you wish, and your family and the people you care about most will receive what you want them to receive.

Now, this kind of planning might sound different to you than the exciting world of stock market investments. Some financial professionals don't do holistic planning—they simply don't have the qualifications. Others can sell you life insurance policies to protect your family, but they don't have the licenses they need to sell market investments. You might have heard different terms such as financial advisors, investment advisors, financial planners, and brokers. So what's the difference?

WHAT IF YOU ALREADY HAVE AN ADVISOR?

The description *financial advisor* is very general, and a lot of people call themselves *advisors* even if they don't offer holistic advice that includes all asset classes and financial concerns such as Social Security, taxes, and estate planning. This makes it tricky for the average consumer to figure out what kind of expert they're working with and what kinds of services they offer.

Just as a square is a rectangle, but a rectangle isn't a square, a lot of investment advisors are financial advisors, but not all financial advisors are investment advisors. Confused yet? I don't blame you.

Here's an easy way to figure out if you're working with the right person. Basically, every investor goes through three financial phases in their life: accumulation, preservation, and distribution. (See Chapter 11: Stages of Your Financial Life.) An investment adviser representative (IAR) has the training, licenses, and qualifications to help you during all three of those phases, no matter which one you happen to be in. This may not be the case for other kinds of financial professionals.

---

5 https://www.nytimes.com/2015/05/09/your-money/some-new-math-for-the-4-percent-retirement-rule.html

WHY YOU WANT TO WORK WITH AN INVESTMENT ADVISOR REPRESENTATIVE

The first two parts of the EDED plan—the logbook and the 10/20/70 budget—help you get a handle on where your money is going so you can eliminate debt and start saving. Once you've established enough savings, you might wonder: **how can I invest my savings so that the money I've saved can work for me to increase my savings even more?** Great question.

In 2015, the founder of Retirement Researcher and Professor of Retirement Income Wade Pfau looked at recent research in an attempt to quantify how good financial advice can help an investor who is trying to save money. The research focused on the areas of tax efficiency, investment fees, risk management, and the value of good investment decisions. **What they found was that investors who worked with investment advisor representatives earned on average 3 percent more than investors who were managing the money on their own.**[6] What's more, that 3 percent is what they earned *after* paying the advisor fee.

After spending some time in the financial industry, including some time selling life insurance, I made what was perhaps the most important decision of my career: the decision to become an investment adviser representative. I earned this license in addition to maintaining a license to sell insurance. My objective was and still is to offer clients a holistic planning service that takes into account all the phases of an investor's life and all of the key aspects of financial planning. For me, this comes in three parts, which also speaks to the different kinds of financial professionals you're likely to meet:

Securities. Technically, the title of "investment advisor" was made official with the passage of the Investment Advisors Act of 1940, a law created in response to the wildly bad advice being proffered during the stock market surge in the Roaring Twenties. We all know how that ended, with a crash that wiped out billions of dollars, destroyed the lives and savings of countless people, and

---

6   https://retirementresearcher.com/the-value-of-financial-advice/

triggered the Great Depression. At that point, our lawmakers decided that something had to be done to ensure investors had the opportunity to access investment counsel that took their interests into consideration, so they created the job of "investment advisor" to draw a line in the sand: on one side were the traditional brokers, focused on generating sales, and on the other were investment advisors, focused on providing investment advice as part of an overall financial plan.

A lot has changed in the many decades since that law was passed (see "What's Fiduciary Got to Do with It?") but the distinction remains important. I chose to become an investment advisor representative because when I provide securities advice, it is always a part of my clients' whole, coordinated financial plan.

Accumulation is one of the three phases of financial life, as we'll discuss in Chapter 11, but it is also a critical strategy in every financial plan at every stage. Securities are one very popular and effective tool to achieve that accumulation, and as such, I wanted to be able to offer my clients the best advice possible in this area.

Flat-fee vs. commission. The question you need to ask yourself about a financial professional is this: who does this person really work for? Brokers often work for themselves or for the company who pays their salary and bonus money. They sell various investment products (or insurance products) and earn commissions based on those sales. If there is a certain investment that you need, brokers working for captive companies may only be able to offer you a selection of the investments sold by their company. Even if their investment has much higher fees than comparative investments, they aren't required to tell you that. Instead, they say, "I have this really great investment here," and you sign the paperwork, and they collect their commission.

I am both an investment adviser representative and an insurance broker. As an IAR, I work on a fee-only basis. Here's why that matters ... Commission-based brokers earn differing amounts of money depending on which products they sell; flat-fee brokers earn a percentage of their clients' assets under management, which puts them squarely on their clients' teams. It's in their best interest, basically, to do what's in your best interest: to make you the most money.

Like many investment adviser representatives, I own and operate my own firm. I don't work for a large company, because I want to be able to offer my clients a choice of investments that are in their best interest, instead of in the best interest of the company. This means I'm not restricted to certain company brands.

A word about financial planners. "Financial planner" is a very general term for anyone who helps clients create a financial plan. In this sense I am both a financial planner and an investment adviser representative, but I don't typically call myself a planner for one key reason: it can mean a lot of different things. It doesn't require a specific certification or exam; it doesn't even indicate a particular set of services. A financial planner might or might not be licensed to sell securities or insurance solutions—they might even be trained in doing so. There are "Certified Financial Planners®" or CFP®s, financial professionals

WHAT'S FIDUCIARY GOT TO DO WITH IT?

A financial professional who is held to a "fiduciary standard" is legally obligated to put his or her clients' interests first, and to avoid conflicts of interest that could interfere with the clients' best interests. That fiduciary standard is inherently connected to some financial professionals. In fact, one of the reasons I chose to become an investment adviser representative is because we are held to the fiduciary standard. It's important that my clients know that I put them first at all times, and that I'm completely transparent about fees, commissions, and motives. The fiduciary standard is also the reason I chose to be a fee-only investment advisor, because commissions can present a potential conflict of interest.

The issue of which professionals should be held to a fiduciary standard is one that has been hotly debated by our government. *It's been estimated that middle-class investors and working-class families pay a total of $17 billion every year in unnecessary backdoor payments and hidden fees to advisors NOT held to this standard.*[1] If keeping more of your money is important to you—and it should certainly be

1 https://obamawhitehouse.archives.gov/the-press-office/2015/02/23/fact-sheet-middle-class-economics-strengthening-retirement-security-crac

who are examined and certified by the Center for Financial Planning Board of Standards, Inc.

There are plenty of excellent financial planners out there, of course. Whether or not a particular planner is "excellent" for you

something you consider—ask any financial professional you're considering (or already working with) if they are legally bound to a fiduciary standard. You should always ask how they get paid as well.

depends on a lot of things, including their expertise, experience, training, and services offered, but also, your financial phase and your personal preferences and goals. It's important, once again—you'll read this advice from me a lot—to do your own homework, ask the right questions, and hold your financial professional to a high standard.

Find a Professional Who Works for YOU

One of the most common things I see among new clients working with commission-based financial professionals is that they don't know what fees they are paying. One of the services I offer to all new clients is called a Portfolio X-Ray®. This sophisticated software tool created by Morningstar runs an analysis of your portfolio so that we can both see exactly where you are at. It's oftentimes a 60-page printout that shows every fee in addition to the risk analysis. This can be very helpful when determining which investments should be moved in order to capitalize on better gains.

New clients tend to be very surprised when I run these reports and analyses for them, or when I bring up other areas such as timing their Social Security benefits, or planning for long-term care, or diversifying their taxes. "My other financial advisor doesn't do all this," they tell me. "If I have a tax question, he tells me to go ask my tax guy."

This is perhaps the biggest reason to work with an investment adviser representative, or a professional who operates a registered investment advisory firm. They will often have partnerships in place, as I do, with CPAs, legal attorneys, Medicare specialists, or third-party money managers; they will have the licenses needed to get you into stocks, bonds, or life insurance products. They will be able to grow your money or protect your money, manage your assets or help you distribute them in the most efficient manner possible. This kind of robust financial planning is why an investment adviser representative may be able to give you a more productive portfolio, one that relies on tactical management versus passive strategies, and integrates all your financial decisions together. This may allow you to do more with what you have, without having to assume more risk.

Make an Investment in Yourself

I've said it before, but it's so important that I'll probably repeat it a few more times: in order to change your life, you have to change your beliefs first, and you can only do that through action. When I was a kid, I believed that some people just didn't make enough money to save. I believed that when you came from my part of town, or from my family specifically, hard work that never really got you anywhere was just the way of life. When I finally got a little money—because I was, after all, a hard worker—I spent more of it than I had. The world makes it easy to do that, throwing credits cards and loans at anyone who can keep a job for more than a few weeks.

The world makes it easy for you to fail. Only you can make the decisions that lead to success.

When my Jeep was repossessed, I was so ashamed that I decided, even though I didn't really believe I could do better, that I would have to try. I couldn't stand the alternative. And so I began my logbook. Then I started my 10/20/70 budget. Before long, those small actions led to big changes in my debts and in my bank accounts, and even more importantly, in my beliefs. The greater the changes I created, the more my confidence grew, and I knew I could achieve even more.

What if I could help someone else like me, to show them with my story and my methods that their beliefs and their lives could change?

That's what I decided to do, and that's why I became not just a financial advisor, but one who is committed to providing my clients with all of the services they need to create a successful financial plan—a plan that will serve them for their lifetimes. I also decided to charge a flat fee, so that I only succeed when my clients succeed.

Whomever you decide to hire as your professional, make that the standard: *your financial professional needs, first and foremost, to work for you.* You need someone who believes that you can succeed, and you deserve to work with someone who is equipped to help make that happen.

Before Moving On
to the Next Chapter:

At this point, the logbook should be a strong habit, and you should be using your 10/20/70 budget. Your debt should be shrinking, and your savings should be growing. That's great progress, so first, you should pat yourself on the back and keep up the good work.

Depending on where you are in the process, you might need to spend more time:

- Focusing on paying down debt

- Building up your emergency fund

- Building up the savings you'd like to invest

Or perhaps you are ready to start investing.

Regardless of which of those statements describes you, there's one thing every reader can and should do before moving on to the next chapter, and that's to start looking for the right financial professional. You might not be ready to hire someone right away, but now is a good time to start considering what is important to you. Consider the questions below, and start making a list of what you want in a financial professional. When you start shopping for one, you'll be ready.

- What kind of services (e.g. securities, insurance, Medicare planning, etc.) are important to you?

- What certifications and licenses are important to you?

- What types of clients do you want your financial professional to specialize in (e.g. young professionals, retirees, etc.)?

- Do any of your family members or friends have financial professionals they trust whom you might consider? If so, are these professionals held to the fiduciary standard?

- What kind of pay structure (fee-only or commission-based) do you want your financial professional to use?

- What kind of investment philosophy do you want your financial professional to have? Are you looking for someone who specializes in certain kinds of investments?

- Do you want a financial professional who will work with you directly or are you okay working with a firm, in which your account is managed by a team of financial professionals?

- Do you want a financial professional who is local and can meet with you in person?

- How often do you want to meet with your financial professional? Some professionals meet with their clients annually, while others prefer biannually or quarterly meetings (or at least are open to them if you would prefer to meet more often)?

- What kind of communication do you expect from a financial professional? Do you want monthly updates? Annual ones? Do you prefer email communication or phone calls?

Chapter 9:
INVESTING FOR THE FUTURE

If you would become wealthy, then what you save must earn, and its children must earn, that all may help to give to you the abundance you crave.

~ George S. Clason, *The Richest Man in Babylon*

Wealth. That's a word that means a lot of different things to different people. For me, for the purposes of *Every Dime, Every Day*, wealth means *abundance*, and not just an abundance of zeros at the end of your bank balance. **True wealth is an abundance of peace of mind**. Having enough money to care for your needs and your family's needs can certainly provide that, but true abundance also speaks to so many other things. Depending on your goals, it could mean an abundance of time to be with your family, an abundance of joy in the work you get to do every day, or abundant freedom to pursue your dreams. You get the idea. Abundant peace of mind can only be good.

With the logbook and the 10/20/70 rule, you learned two things: first, where your money is going, and second, how to *control* where your money goes. Now—congratulations—you've got some savings! But while savings are fantastic, saving alone isn't enough to achieve an abundance of wealth or peace or whatever your goals might be. In order to achieve that and ensure your abundance isn't temporary, you have to put those savings to work for you. In this chapter, we're going to talk about *how*.

How Much Do I Need to Start Investing?

This is a great question, and like many great questions, it has a lot of different answers. But there are some helpful guidelines.

Emergency fund. Before you consider investing, you need to build up an emergency fund. The common advice is to have enough savings in your emergency fund to pay for at least three months of expenses. The good news is that, thanks to your logbook, you know exactly what three months of expenses will cost! The bad news: that might not be enough. Exactly how much you need in an emergency fund depends on a lot of things, including your comfort level and your employment situation.

Retirement saving. You might already be investing. If you have an employer-sponsored 401(k), you should be making whatever contribution is required to get your employer's maximum match. If your employer offers up to a 6 percent match, for example, you should be contributing 6 percent of each paycheck to your 401(k). That's *doubling* your retirement savings for free. Why wouldn't you do that if you can?

Investing. Once you have an emergency fund that meets your specific needs and comfort level, then you can start thinking about other investment options. Exactly how much money you need to start investing depends on what kind of investments you want to make.

Investments as Part of Your Financial Plan

When you've found the right financial professional, it will be time to start structuring your financial plan. The thing is, there is no one financial plan that works for everyone. The right financial plan will be targeted to:

Your specific financial situation (which changes as you make progress)

Your specific financial goals (which change as you achieve previous financial goals)

Your financial stage of life (which changes as you age)

In a nutshell: your plan has to fit YOU. How much you invest and what you choose to invest in will change over time along with all of those factors. This is because of one tricky little aspect of investing: risk.

The general wisdom of investing holds that the greater the risk, the greater your potential for return. While this is true in some senses (the stock market offers the potential for some of the greatest returns in investing, but it can just as easily tank, and take your savings with it), there are also certain investments that may provide higher returns without requiring an excessive level of risk.

First Priority: Emergency Savings

Before you decide on any investments, you will need to determine how much of your savings you want to invest. Here's where we get to one of the few things in financial planning that is true for everyone: **you must have an emergency fund.** How much money you need in that emergency fund differs for everyone, but an often-used standard is three months of expenses—enough money to pay all of your essential bills—in some kind of liquid account. Liquidity refers to how accessible your money is. Some investments are designed for the long term, and so they assess penalties if you try to cash them in early; other investments carry risk, and so you might have to take a loss if you sell at the wrong time. If your emergency fund isn't totally liquid, then you might have to pay for the privilege of spending your own cash, and this is never a good thing.

So where should your emergency fund be located so that it's liquid and safe? This is a good use for a **savings account**. These days, savings accounts generally do not deliver much in the way of interest rates currently. When you want liquidity and safety, you have to give up the potential for growth. Sure, it would be nice for your emergency fund to grow, but accumulation isn't the point of an emergency fund.

Another option for your emergency fund that delivers a slightly higher potential for growth is a **money market account**. It still offers liquidity and safety, but with an interest rate that is typically a little higher than that of a regular savings account. The tradeoff is that you typically need a larger deposit to qualify for these rates. Also, money market accounts can require you to give up a little liquidity. Just like savings accounts, money market accounts are subject to the Federal Reserve's "Regulation D," which means that you can only make a limited number of withdrawals per month—six, to be exact. However, because of the higher interest rates offered by money market accounts, many banks limit those allowed withdrawals even further. If you plan on using a money market account as an emergency fund, be sure to understand all of the limitations on the account you choose.

RETIREMENT SAVING

HOW MUCH SHOULD I SAVE?

The answer to this question depends on your needs and wants, the kind of lifestyle you hope to have in retirement, and the kinds of things you want to do. For a lot of people, the goal is to have a $1 million retirement nest egg. Experts suggest that while $1 million sounds like plenty, it's really probably only enough for one person, not enough to cover a spouse. So, if you're married, you each want to try to reach that $1 million retirement savings. That's a big number, $1 million, I know, so let's break down exactly what that means in terms of how much you have to save and when.

Thanks to the wonder of compound interest, if you're young, time is on your side. The earlier you start investing, the more time your money will have to compound, or grow exponentially. Let's say you're 25 years old. You only have to save $15 a day and invest it in a portfolio earning an average 6 percent return to hit that million-dollar mark by age 67.

It sounds fantastic, but remember: the longer you wait to save, the less time you'll have for compound interest to help you. That means make a plan and start today. You're losing money every day you put it off.

HOW MUCH RISK?

With your emergency fund safely tucked away (but easily accessible), the rest of your savings can be invested. So how much risk is the right amount for you? This is where the Rule of 100 comes in.

The Rule of 100 is a simple way to determine how much of your savings should be at risk depending on your age. It's based on the idea that you should be taking more risk when you're younger, enabling your money to grow faster during the time of your life when you don't need those savings. As you get closer to retirement and the time that you will need that money, most people want to reduce the amount of risk their savings are exposed to. The Rule of 100 goes like this:

- 100 – your age = the percentage of your savings that should be at risk

- For example, 100 – 35 = 65, so 35-year-olds should have 65 percent of their savings at risk.

- But 100 − 65 = 35, so 65-year-olds should only have 35 percent of their money at risk.

This is a general rule to help guide you, but you also have to be comfortable with your risk level regardless of this rule. For some people, the idea of putting any amount of their savings at risk is just too stressful, so lower-risk investments are preferable even when they're younger. Other people get a thrill from investing and simply want to take more risk. If you have enough assets to do this without threatening your lifestyle, then you can consider taking on more risk.

WHICH INVESTMENTS?

Once you know how much of your savings you want to invest and the amount of risk you're willing and able to take, you're ready to consider which kinds of investments to buy. Your financial professional should discuss all of your options with you, as well as a concept called *diversification*. Although a long word, the concept is relatively simple: basically, you don't want to have all of your eggs in one basket. When investing, it's a good idea to have some variety in your holdings, so that if one category of the economy takes a nosedive, you don't run the risk of watching all your money go with it.

Here are some of the major investment types you might consider:

Stocks. These are types of securities, and as such, you're putting your money 100 percent at risk with these investments. With a stock, you're buying a piece of a company in the hope that the company will grow and do well. You earn money either from dividends paid to stock owners or by selling that stock if it has increased in value. Generally speaking, stocks are very liquid investments; when you want your money back, you simply sell (hopefully for a profit).

Bonds. A bond is like a loan; a company or government sells bonds to finance a project, and you earn interest over the specific period of time that you loan them the money. There are several risks with bonds, including the potential that the bond's interest rate won't keep pace with inflation, and the possibility that the borrower won't be able to pay back the loan. Some bonds, such as U.S. Treasury bonds, are considered risk-free in terms of payback, but they also earn low interest rates, and you give up your access to liquidity, usually for a period of years.

Investment funds. Investment funds allow investors with common goals to pool together their savings so that they can benefit from larger investments and lower individual risk. One of the most common types of investment funds are mutual funds. These give you a simplified way to diversify among stocks and bonds, but there are downsides. Mutual funds may be expensive due to loads, operating expenses, and 12b-1 fees. For example, front-end loads are commissions or sales charges immediately deducted from your initial deposit, so whatever you think you are investing starts out lower right away. Another downside is that they trade only at the close of the market, but the client is typically informed and given an assured closing price. There is another type of investment fund that has surged in popularity over the last few years: exchange-traded funds (ETFs). ETFs give you the same ability to pool and diversify your savings, but they typically have lower operating expenses, no loads, and no 12b-1 fees. They also typically give you greater access to liquidity than mutual funds because they trade just like a stock—trading throughout the day—rather than only at the close of the market.

Retirement accounts. Accounts such as 401(k)s and IRAs (both Roth and non-Roth versions) offer ways for you to invest your money for retirement. The money you contribute to these accounts is invested for you, either by a fund manager, which is common in employer-sponsored programs like 401(k)s, or by you or your investment professional, as in an IAR. Your money is at risk in these funds, as they are typically invested in securities like stocks and mutual funds, and they each operate by specific tax rules. Be sure you understand exactly what the tax consequences are and what restrictions may apply.

Real estate. This is one of the less traditional investments, but it's one to consider. Real estate has played a big role in my financial plan, and it can be an excellent way to put your savings to work for you. In my many years of real estate investing, I've bought dozens of properties and turned them into rental properties. I've found that I prefer real estate investing because it's a real, physical thing that you can see, touch, and control.

There are other ways to invest in real estate beyond buying rental properties. Other options include real estate investment funds, which are a kind of mutual fund that invests in stocks offered by real estate corporations, and REITs (real estate investment trusts), which are companies or trusts that own real estate that produces income, allowing it to pay dividends to shareholders.

Insurance products. Cash value life insurance is an insurance product sometimes used as an investment. Unlike term life insurance, which is more like renting your insurance for a short period of time, cash value life insurance is bought, paid for, and lasts your entire lifetime. When you pay premiums on cash value life insurance, you earn equity like you do in a home or other asset. As such, cash value life insurance policies are much more expensive than term policies, and while they can provide a good investment tool for the right circumstances, those circumstances are very specific.

There are also some products offered by insurance companies that can provide growth as well as insurance. Annuities are one of the most common insurance investment products on the market, but they aren't always offered to investors. An annuity is a contract between you and an insurance company: you give the insurance company a sum of money, and in exchange that insurance company promises to make periodic payments to you. Annuities are guaranteed by the insurance company that sells them, so their risk depends on the claims-paying ability of the insurance company. Depending on the type of annuity, returns can be low to moderate.

THE THREE BASIC TYPES OF ANNUITIES

A lot of investment advisors and brokers might not bring the annuity to the table because of revenue. They may or may not make as much money selling annuities as they do with managed accounts. This is where working with a fiduciary who is looking out for your best interest might be vital to the stability of your portfolio. An annuity may be a better fit for the investor who is at or nearing the time of retirement, and so it might be worth giving these products a second look.

Because there are so many different types of annuities, people often think they know about them all, when really, they only know something about one type. Annuities are kind of like fruit: to say that you hate all fruit because you don't like bananas would mean missing out on all the good berries and melons of the world. Whether you think these are good investments or bad investments, let's take a minute to understand what they are, what they can do, and when or if one might be a good fit for part of your investment portfolio.

Fixed annuities are the simplest and the easiest to understand. They earn a fixed interest rate for a set period of time, usually five years. In a portfolio, they can compete with five-year bank CDs, and in today's world, these annuities can get you rates north of 3 percent. Rates vary based on what's available and market conditions. A fixed annuity might be a good choice for someone in their 70s who wants something with a better rate than a CD account. They can give your portfolio some safety and principal protection, but the downside is you cannot access the principal for a set period of years, so liquidity is limited. However, you CAN usually access the interest every year, as most annuities allow you to make 10 percent withdrawals without penalties or fees.

Variable annuities are on the other side of the spectrum, and they are the most complicated and expensive kinds of annuities that you can own. They earn interest through securities that are invested in the stock market, so they do expose your money to market risk. They also have the ability to turn your money into a stream of income. This kind of two-for-one investment comes with a hefty price tag. If you're going to invest in the stock market, you might be better off working with an advisor who can try to get you into a low-cost investment account rather than investing in an expensive variable annuity. If your goal is to turn your savings into a stream of income, almost any annuity is better than the variable kind because of the high risk and fees.

This is often a confusing issue when working with a financial advisor, especially if they are working for a name-brand company. They will likely use terms like "proprietary investments" and make it sound as if their annuity is the best one out there and the only one that can get you good returns. Please be advised that annuities are long-term commitments. It's like getting hitched: before saying "I do" to any annuity, I strongly suggest that you take the time to get a second opinion from an investment adviser representative who has your best interest in mind. If you already have an annuity and you're not sure what kind it is, ask the IAR to review it for you. He or she will be able to run reports and uncover any hidden fees.

Fixed-indexed annuities (sometimes called FIAs) were designed to give you the best of both the fixed annuity and the variable. As their name suggests, they are part of the fixed family, but they also have the ability to index. This allows you to participate in the upside of market gains without exposing your nest egg to the full effects of downside loss. The FIA can offer principal protection, but there is a trade-off: these market-linked gains are typically capped. For example, if the index gained 10 percent and the cap rate was 8 percent, then the gain in your annuity would be 8 percent. Unlike a variable annuity, however, you don't have to pay underlying fund expenses because FIAs do not directly invest in securities, and some FIAs have NO fees built right into the contract.

In my opinion, there are basically two ways you can use an FIA. If you want to lower market risk from a portion of your portfolio, you might take an amount of money, park it inside an FIA, and let it grow for five to 10 years where it will earn indexed returns without direct exposure to market loss. Using the Rule of 100, this might be a good idea for someone who is in their 60s, for example, looking to put a percentage of their money into a fixed spot. Instead of going to a bond portfolio where you would still have market risk based on interest rates, you can choose the FIA because it can give you competitive rates—at least what a bond portfolio would pay—while offering you principal protection. At the end of the designated time period, your contract will have expired, and you can take that money out of the annuity and do whatever you want with it, potentially with no penalties and no strings attached.

The second way you can use an FIA is for income planning. Like any annuity, they have the ability to turn a sum of money into a lifetime stream of income. FIAs offer some of the most flexible options for income streams, allowing you to get a pension-like paycheck from a portion of your portfolio, guaranteed by the claims-paying ability of the insurance company. If you work with an investment advisor who is independent and not tied to using certain investments from any one company, they will be able to shop around from different insurance companies to give you an annuity with the best terms, rates, and strongest guarantees. Obviously, because of the long-term commitment and limited access to liquidity, you probably wouldn't want to put the bulk of your portfolio into an annuity. A fiduciary working in your best interest can help you figure out what portion of your portfolio might be best served by which type of annuity, and they can help you choose one from an insurance company that will best fit your needs.

TAX CONSIDERATIONS

Anytime you earn income, you know what's not far behind: taxes. Investments are no different. They can be, however, a bit more complex than your average W-2. Since everyone's situation is unique, it's always a good idea to work with a tax professional when you begin investing, but here are a few things you need to consider as well:

Tax-deferred accounts. Some investment accounts, such as 401(k) s and IRAs, are tax-deferred, allowing you to contribute pre-tax money so that you can pump up your balance and supercharge the power of your compounding interest. With these accounts, you pay taxes at the time of withdrawal. That is preferable for many retirees, since their income tax bracket is often lower during retirement than during their working years, but it's something you need to plan for.

Capital gains. The goal of investing is to make money, but when you do, you'll also have to pay taxes on those gains. In the case of securities, when you sell one and make a profit, the kind of tax you pay is called "capital gains tax." But you can pay less in those capital gains taxes if you know what you're doing. For example, if you own your investment for more than 12 months, then the tax rate you pay is lower (as of this writing).

Dividend taxes. You'll also need to pay taxes on dividends you earn from your investments, but be aware that the dividends from some investments are taxed at a lower rate than others, and still others aren't taxed at all. In some cases, dividends earned from municipal bonds are tax-exempt on your federal returns.

Taxes can be complex, and these are just some of the primary tax considerations you need to keep in mind when you add investing to your financial plan. The bottom line, though, is not that you need to *pay* your taxes differently, but instead that you need to change the way you *approach* your taxes. Until now, chances are pretty good that you approached your taxes like most people: you reported them.

Somewhere around April, you added up all the things you earned and paid in the previous year, figured out if the IRS needed to give you a refund or if you still owed more taxes, and you submitted that return.

But now things are different. Now you have a financial plan. And tax planning is always part of effective financial planning. That means that instead of just paying taxes based on what happened last year, you look ahead and consider how your financial decisions will affect what taxes you owe. Every dollar that you don't have to pay in taxes is a dollar that can go into your savings and toward your future. Those dollars can earn for you, which is why you want to incorporate tax strategies into your financial plan.

Before Moving on to the Next Chapter:

Whether you're ready to begin making actual investments or not, it's never too soon to start planning. With the help of a trusted financial professional, you can make investment decisions that best fit your circumstances and goals, but remember: you're in charge. As the person in charge, you'd better start thinking about what you want right now, even if you're not quite ready to move money into investments. Before moving on, it's time to prepare yourself by thinking about the conversations you'll need to have with your financial professional before making any major moves.

How much money do you need in an emergency savings account to feel safe and comfortable? Use your logbook to see how much you spend each month and then consider your job situation. How long do you think it would take to find a new job if yours was suddenly gone? Or, what if you got sick? Do you have disability insurance that could help cover your expenses (or your part of them)? All of these considerations should go into your decision about just how much emergency savings is enough.

When you have your emergency savings put away safely, you're ready to consider investing. What investment types are appealing to you?

Research some investments that you might like to include in your plan. Make a list of those investments and answer the following questions for each:

What goal do I believe this investment will help me achieve?

- How long will my money need to stay in this investment to be profitable?

- What are the penalties and/or disadvantages if I take my money out before that time?

- How quickly would it be possible to get my money back if necessary? (Though you shouldn't invest money that you need immediately: that's what a healthy emergency fund is for.)

- What company or individual would I be buying this investment from? What is the reputation and outlook for that entity?

- Is this an investment product that is registered with the SEC and/or a state agency?

- What fees will I pay with this investment? How often will I pay them?

- Is this a low-, moderate-, or high-risk investment?

In the next chapter, we'll talk more about how investments can turbocharge your savings, and you'll have the chance to think more about the specific types of investments you might want to include in your overall investment plan. You've come a long way already and made amazing transformations in how you manage your money. Take some time to congratulate yourself, and then keep reading, and keep an eye on those dimes every day!

Chapter 10:
TURBOCHARGE YOUR SAVINGS

*Beware of little expenses; a small leak
will sink a great ship.*

~ Benjamin Franklin

Seed money is a business term that refers to the money raised to start a new company or cause. Investors give the new enterprise a certain amount of money in exchange for some stake in the company—part ownership, profit sharing, etc. Are you wondering why we're talking about seed money? This isn't a book about starting a new business, is it? You're right. It's not. But then again, it is. You are your own business. You and your family are your most important cause. People who run their homes like businesses are far more successful than people who do not. So, let's get back to seed money.

When I started EDED, I was just trying to get out of debt. I didn't really believe yet that I would ever have enough savings to invest. Deciding what to invest in was a problem I only dreamed of having. I didn't believe I'd ever have enough to invest. Quickly enough, though, I started to see that my everyday actions of keeping the logbook and sticking to my 10/20/70 plan made significant changes in both my debt and in my savings—changes that started to add up. Soon, I was thinking of my household as a business and our savings as seed money. Just like people sketching their startup dreams out on a napkin, Erika and I would discuss what our lives could be like if we committed to investing in ourselves like we might a business. If we could increase our seed money, our profits could grow faster. And who would get all those profits? Us. As the sole investors in our little enterprise, we would reap all the rewards.

Investing is how you put your money to work on your behalf, sending it out into the world to make money for you. But the more you can invest—the more seed money you contribute—the greater those earnings can be.

Now that you've got your logbook habit down and your 10/20/70 plan firmly in place, what if we changed that plan a bit? What if we tried to make it more like 20/20/60? What if you could save even more? What if you could save 30 percent? 40 percent? It might sound impossible. Believe me, if I hadn't done it, I wouldn't believe it. But in our very early days of marriage and parenthood, Erika and I found ways to turbocharge our savings and increase our seed money. In some of those years, even years when our income was modest, we found ways to save as much as 50 percent of our income.

We weren't working from an inheritance. We didn't have super-high-paying jobs. We simply found ways to economize and save a little extra. You can do it too.

LOOK FOR WAYS TO SAVE MORE

Every Dime, Every Day isn't about gimmicks. Shortcuts won't make you rich just like they won't make you skinny or healthy. Everyone knows that you can only stay on the cabbage diet for so long before you run screaming out of the house to get a big, juicy burger. Learning to make yourself wealthy is just the same: it's about changing habits and lifestyle, about finding balance, making sacrifices but also rewarding yourself in meaningful ways that will keep you motivated.

That said, there are some savings shortcuts that can help you beef up that seed money and reach your savings goals faster. That's what this chapter is all about.

Review your insurance. This is something you can do with that trusted financial professional you've found. When I work with new clients, I always review their insurance coverage to be sure that they aren't double or triple covered and paying for things they don't need. More often than not, they are. You'd be surprised how much you can save when you take a serious look at all of the coverage you carry and eliminate redundant coverage. We're talking hundreds of dollars per month for some people. Now, be careful: I'm not saying you should cut insurance that you do need. I'm saying work with a professional who can help you really examine what kind of coverage you need, what kind you have, and what can be cut because you either don't need it or are already paying for it in another policy.

Be thrifty. My wife coupons. Even today, Erika loves to see how much she can save with coupons. I'm not so into the couponing—though she is amazing at it, saves us a ton, and I'm grateful she enjoys it—but I do love to see how I can get something I want or need for a little (or a lot!) less. There are ways to do this without couponing, by the way. Buying things secondhand is a great one. My family lives in Maine, where having a snowmobile can be both useful and fun. But why would we need the newest, fanciest, most expensive model? We could spend almost $13,000 on a brand-new one, or find the same model that's just a couple of years old and pay almost half that. That's $6,000 or so that can go into our seed money while we still reward ourselves with an exciting new toy.

Don't increase your lifestyle spending when your income increases. This one is hard for a lot of people. You get that big raise, and you tell yourself, I deserve to enjoy this. And you do. You deserve a reward for sure. But you also deserve the bigger things that your raise can give you. You deserve to focus on achieving your goals, like paying down debt or building savings that can give you financial freedom, even faster. When your income increases, look at your entire financial picture. Your logbook will make this very simple. Plan for a reward that will allow you to enjoy your achievement and put the rest of your increased earnings toward savings.

Pay less in taxes. Hold on—I'm not suggesting you pay fewer taxes than you legally owe. I am, however, saying that a lot of people pay more taxes than they should, and it's because of a lack of planning and awareness. Working with a Certified Public Accountant (CPA) who is skilled at tax planning might seem like an extra expense that you can just avoid by using some free or cheap tax software, but you're cheating yourself if you think that. If you aren't putting money into a tax-qualified retirement plan (more on that in Chapter 15), then you are paying taxes right now that you could pay later in retirement when your tax rate will probably be much lower. That's not the right strategy for everyone, but if it is the right strategy for you, and you're paying hundreds or even thousands of dollars in taxes that you could be putting into your seed money, wouldn't you want to know? Tax planning is crucial in retirement, by the way, when every distribution you take could cause a huge tax slap, so why not find a trusted CPA or a financial professional who works with a CPA and start tax planning now?

Add some income on the side. If you've exhausted all of the ways you can cut your spending, how about adding some income instead? I'll bet you have things lying around the house you can sell. Just give it some thought. That kayak you haven't used in three years? You can probably live without it. All of that baby stuff you stored in the attic years ago because you just weren't sure what to do with it? Have a yard sale. Or turn to the web. Thanks to the Internet, there are hundreds of easy ways to make some extra cash off the stuff you don't need, but also, you could start a side gig to bring in bonus earnings. When you're out of town, rent your house on a home vacation rental site. Check out other opportunities, such as reposting photos online for cash. There are tons of things out there that you can do to earn extra seed money while you have your feet up.

WHAT HAPPENS TO ALL THAT SEED MONEY?

Just as the name implies, seed money gets planted. It's what you use to invest in whatever options you and your financial professional determine are the best fit for your needs and circumstances. But there is another thing you do for seeds that you must also do for your seed money: protect it.

Beyond all of the traditional investment opportunities that we discussed in the last chapter, there is a whole world of additional opportunities. In some cases, those opportunities are limited to investors who meet certain income criteria. For example, getting in on the ground floor of a startup company, one that's not ready to go public and sell stock yet, is a high-risk but potentially very high-reward way to invest. These startups, who are looking to make their own seed money, might solicit the support of "qualified investors," also known as SEC accredited investors—the only kind of individual the SEC allows companies to solicit for this kind of support. But in order to be one, your individual net worth has to be at least $1 million, or you must make $200,000 per year—or, if you're married, $300,000 with a spouse. Plus, in order to invest that money, you have to not need it for your living expenses. So, safe to say, not all opportunities will be on the table right away.

But a number of Internet venture capital investment platforms have appeared in recent years. These platforms allow investors with much smaller sums of money, even as low as $100, to combine with other investors' money in order to invest in some, but not all (some are still limited to those qualified investors) startups.

These sites aren't the only less-traditional kinds of investments you'll run across. Some people invest in metals, such as gold, in oil or gas futures, or even in collectible items, while others take part in what's called peer-to-peer lending, which is just what it sounds like: offering loans to an individual out of your own pocket.

All of this brings us back to one thing: protect your seed money. You worked hard to save that 10 percent, and now you've worked even harder to turbocharge your savings by increasing your monthly savings even more. Don't put it into the hands of a high-risk investment with no protections.

That doesn't mean you can't get creative. After all, Erika and I have historically invested primarily in real estate, not mutual funds or stocks. We have purchased homes or buildings and then used them as income-generating rental properties, and it's been a wonderful investment for us. There is a lot of risk in real estate investing, and you need some expertise to choose the right buildings that will actually generate income. There are also no protections, as there are with low-risk investments like, for example, CDs, or certificates of deposit (sold by banks), or annuities (sold by insurance companies). Those investments have far less risk, but also less reward. With CDs, interest rates are low enough that their returns often don't keep pace with inflation, and that's a risk all on its own.

See how complicated this becomes? In order to make the best decision for you and your future, I recommend two things: first, work with a trusted financial professional, someone who specializes in the kinds of investments you are interested in; and two, always remember to **seek, verify, then act.**

SEEK is the first step. You should always keep an eye out for investments that are a good fit for you. Just as you should read and explore to expand your mind, you should do the same to expand your knowledge of investment possibilities.

When you find investments that are of interest, it's time to **VERIFY.** This means both working with that trusted investment professional and doing your own homework. What is the history and reputation of the company you're considering investing in? What can you find out about the building you are thinking about purchasing? Are you able to have it inspected? There's no way to give yourself 100 percent protection, but there are things you can do to thoroughly vet any possible investment to ensure you're making the smartest choice.

Then **ACT**. This one is pretty simple. When you feel as though you've fully investigated your potential investment, its pros and cons, its risks and rewards—and ONLY then—you act.

Just as you are cautious about which financial professionals you trust to advise you on your overall financial plan, you should be equally discerning when investing your money. Beware of people who are out to steal your money. They're out there, and they're good at what they do.

Before Moving on to the Next Chapter:

- How can you begin turbocharging your savings? Using the ideas in this chapter and your own research, make a list of all of the possible ways you can increase the amount you are saving each month.

- Set a goal for yourself that feels doable. Maybe it's to save an additional $100 for the next three months or to increase your savings from 10 percent to 15 percent or more. Make this a short-term goal that you can achieve in the next three to six months, and when you achieve it, set an even higher goal.

- Investigate your options for protecting this seed money. Find investment vehicles that you're comfortable with, and do your research. Don't just limit yourself to traditional stock and bond portfolios. Examine things like real estate opportunities and little-known Internet venture capital investment platforms. But be careful: do your homework, and always get a second opinion from an investment adviser representative you trust.

Chapter 11:

STAGES OF YOUR
FINANCIAL LIFE

*A big part of financial freedom is having your heart
and mind free from worry about the what-ifs of life.*

~ Suze Orman

L ike everything else, your financial life will change. There are continuous moments that occur throughout life that alter your financial needs and goals in small and sometimes big ways. That's why financial planning isn't a one-and-done sort of thing. Your financial plan is an ongoing process, one that requires regular attention. A lot of the events that affect your financial plan and goals happen differently or at different times for everyone, but fortunately, we all share three general financial stages:

- Accumulation

- Preservation

- Distribution

Using these stages as our guide, we can be sure that we're addressing all of the critical planning areas regardless of the differing events and timing that make our journeys unique.

ACCUMULATION: AGES 20 TO 50

Accumulation is the stage of your youth. It's when you get your first job, first car, first house. You might get married and begin to include your spouse in your financial goals. You might have kids and add financial goals like planning for their security, care, and education to your list.

Accumulation is also critical. The other two stages of your financial life are built upon the foundation that you lay during Accumulation. For that reason, this is the stage during which, if you have debt, you must focus on paying it down to zero. A lot of people acquire debt in their early 20s. If you can avoid that, then your foundation will already be exponentially stronger.

This is the period of your financial life when you are focused on amassing as much wealth as possible. This is the stage when you build your seed money and you start to invest. You look at investment strategies and make decisions about where to put your money so that it can grow. Because you are putting away money that you won't need for decades, you are able to expose that money to greater risk in exchange for the gains that risk allows you to achieve over the long run. NOTE: That principle doesn't apply to your emergency savings fund. That's the piece of your savings that is liquid and safe. Only your seed money—the money you're growing for retirement—should be invested and exposed to risk.

QUESTIONS TO ASK YOURSELF DURING ACCUMULATION:

What will my tax plan be during retirement? This is the time when you should be earning and saving. A huge part of the purpose of that saving is to provide for your retirement. When starting those savings, you have a number of choices about what kind of retirement savings to choose from, and one of the big things to consider here is taxes. We'll get into greater detail about this decision in Chapter 12: Retire on Your Terms.

What insurance is most appropriate right now? Are you raising a family? If you have a family, then you will want to consider how they will be provided for if anything happens to you. Term life insurance can be a good way to provide protection for your family, to replace your income, to pay off any debts you might have, and to ensure your children and their education are provided for.

How will I take care of my health in retirement? I'm not just talking about health insurance here, although that's important too. I'm also referring to long-term care, which is a specific kind of care, such as in-home, nursing home, or assisted living care. In general, longevity is on the rise—that's the good news—and you can expect to live longer than your parents, probably a lot longer than your grandparents. But with that also comes the need for some assistance or special care, and that's why seven out of 10 people who are 65 and older right now will need long-term care at some point in their lives.[7] Again, we'll discuss this more in the next chapter, but the important thing to know right now is that this isn't a decision to be made when you're at or nearing retirement. It sounds like a retirement decision, but in order to get the best possible options at the best possible rates, you need to decide on a long-term care plan during the Accumulation phase. When you're in your 40s, that's a good time to start thinking about what your needs will be in your 60s and 70s, and plan accordingly.

---

7 http://longtermcare.gov/the-basics/who-needs-care/

Now there are programs that include both life insurance and long-term care planning, which would kill two birds with one stone and possibly save substantial amounts of money over your lifetime. We call this the "new life insurance," a hybrid plan to meet today's needs.

What legal planning should I be doing? Here's the good news: it's unlikely anything is going to happen to you during this phase of your life. But here's the bad news: bad things do happen, and you have to be prepared. You want to protect the people you love, and that's why it's never too early to put together your personal legal plan, which should include

- a will

- a durable power of attorney, which lets you designate someone to make decisions—legal, financial, etc.—for you if you are unable

- an advanced healthcare directive, including a living will that states your wishes for the kind of medical care you would like to receive if you cannot make the decision yourself, and a healthcare power of attorney, which designates someone to make healthcare decisions for you if you are unable.

In some cases, you might also consider setting up a living trust, which can protect your assets to some degree from probate. A trust can also be an appropriate strategy if you are planning for the care of a child with special needs who cannot directly inherit assets. Seek an attorney's advice on all of these documents, but particularly if you are considering a living trust. Many of your assets can be set up so that they do not have to go through probate even without a trust, because setting these up can be an expensive process. It's the right call for certain circumstances, though, and something you should look into carefully.

PRESERVATION: AGES 50 TO 65

Risk is the key word here. The Accumulation stage can be a bit of a roller coaster. You've invested your retirement savings in the market— maybe in mutual funds, stocks, etc.—and you've watched them go up and down, earn and lose. Over the long haul, you've increased those savings, though, but only because you were able to leave that money alone and let it regain any losses. When you enter the Preservation stage, you want to start slowing that roller coaster down. Here's where you start putting on the brakes.

If you still have debt, the Preservation stage is the time to wipe it out for good. You don't want to carry debt into your retirement, when your income and spending money can be less flexible than they have been thus far. If you have a mortgage, you might consider refinancing it during this period, but be careful. In some cases, this can be a good money-saving strategy, but refinancing costs money. There are fees and expenses involved that many people overlook. If your refinanced mortgage doesn't lower your interest rate by two points, then it's probably not saving you any money in the end. Also, don't refinance and then take that extra money and spend it! Put it toward your seed money in savings, and the reward will be much greater in a few years than any purchase could be right now.

The Preservation stage begins about five to 10 years before retirement, depending on your financial circumstances. For most people, this is around ages 50 to 65. You're closing in on the time when you are going to need to start living on those retirement savings you've been carefully building up, and so now you want to start backing off on some of that risk and *preserving* your savings.

QUESTIONS TO ASK YOURSELF DURING PRESERVATION:

NOW what insurance do I need? Are you sensing a trend here? Insurance needs change. Also, insurance can be expensive, so you don't want to be paying for insurance that you don't need. For example, you might have a term life insurance policy you no longer need or a cash value life policy that requires less coverage. This depends on a number of factors, including who is dependent on you and how much financial support you provide for them. It also depends on the assets you have been able to amass. If you have acquired enough assets to provide for your spouse should you pass away, for example, then your life insurance policy could be unnecessary.

Some insurance considerations during Preservation include:

Final expense coverage: Even if you no longer feel you need a big term life insurance policy, you might want to carry a smaller policy to cover final expenses so that your family will not be burdened with those costs.

Spousal continuation: If you're married, you have a partner who is likely dependent, to some degree, on your income. Keep in mind that when one partner passes, expenses don't automatically get cut in half. The mortgage remains the same. So do the utilities. Also, while the two of you would have been living off two Social Security checks, in addition to your other assets, your spouse will only receive the higher of those two checks after you pass. For that reason, you want to consider spousal continuation in every aspect of your financial planning. If you have a pension that includes an option for paying your spouse after you pass, consider that. You might also include insurance policies or insurance products, such as an annuity, to provide income security for your spouse.

Have I reallocated my risk? Too many people pass right through this stage and make no changes to the risk their assets are exposed to. A lot of people found out what a big mistake that can be in the downturn of 2008. Sadly, I met with far too many people who were looking forward to retiring in five or 10 years and then suddenly, they lost 20 percent of their life savings and those dreams were changed.

This kind of devastating loss only happens when someone is asleep at the wheel. Either a person has no financial advisor to alert them to the danger they're in, or that advisor, for whatever reason, decides to let it ride. Either way, if you're just hoping your financial advisor is paying attention, don't. If you aren't hearing anything from your professional about preservation, they probably aren't paying attention. In fact, in this stage, sometimes the most important move you can make is to change financial professionals.

Many times I've seen pre-retirees who have worked with Accumulation specialists for the last couple of decades, and they don't realize they need to make the change to someone who specializes in preservation and retirement. That's not to say that a financial professional can't excel at advising people during all the stages of their financial life. In my experience, it's just that it's not all that common. Unless you are working with an investment adviser representative (IAR), your retirement, security, and comfort might be at risk. This is one area where you want to be sure.

Reallocation isn't something that you do once in your 50s, either. You should work with a financial professional to reexamine your situation, your risk tolerance, etc. and reallocate your assets on a regular basis, ideally every year.

DISTRIBUTION: AGES 65 AND BEYOND

Congratulations! When you arrive at the Distribution stage, it's time to enjoy the fruits of all your labor. I hope you've been following the EDED plan and rewarding yourself for your hard work along the way, but during Distribution, you should start to feel like life is less work and more reward. During this stage, you want to take all of the assets you have amassed and use them to generate income for your retirement. Think of it like this: you've been stockpiling fuel for decades, and now it's time to build an engine to put that fuel into so the engine can take you anywhere you want to go during retirement, safely and comfortably.

QUESTIONS TO ASK YOURSELF
DURING DISTRIBUTION:

How much income will I need? The "engine" of your retirement is your income plan. It's built by first considering any steady sources of income you already have, which, for most people will be Social Security. Pensions can be part of this as well, if you're lucky enough to have one. With that income number firmly in mind, you must then take a look at your monthly income needs. This will be simple since you've been keeping an EDED logbook all these years, right? If you're reading this, and you're already in the Distribution stage, it's time to get very serious about your logbook and focus on your spending. You need to know exactly how much income you need every month.

Next, you take that monthly income need and subtract your reliable income (Social Security and/or pension). Whatever amount is left over is your **income gap**. For example, let's say you are going to receive $1,350 per month from Social Security, and your logbook tells you that you need $2,500 per month in income. That means you have a $1,150 income gap. But don't worry! That's what your assets are for. You will work with your financial professional to put a plan in place that uses your saved assets to generate that $1,150 income. More on that in the next chapter too!

Understandably, one of the biggest concerns for American retirees is running out of money. Creating an income plan that will generate the income you need while preserving the assets that generate the income is not a simple task. That is why working with a financial professional who is experienced at retirement planning is such a crucial factor in having a successful Distribution stage.

How much risk are my assets facing? We've talked a bit about market risk and the need to reallocate your assets during the Preservation stage, but there are other risks to consider during Distribution as well. Remember that retirees are living longer, and the average retiree today lives 20-plus years.[8] That means your assets face the risk of losing buying power to inflation too.

---

8   https://www.ssa.gov/planners/lifeexpectancy.html

Have I put the proper legal instructions in place? If you haven't yet, now is the time to put all of your wishes in writing correctly and legally. Even if you did this in your 30s or 40s or 50s, revisit it. It's not uncommon for your wishes to change. You'd be surprised how many people accidentally leave their ex-wife or ex-husband as the beneficiary on their 401(k), and then their kids (or new spouse) face a surprise when Mom or Dad passes away.

THE JOURNEY AND THE DESTINATION

You hear all the time that life is about the journey, not the destination, but in the case of your finances, it's about both. The destination, whatever that might be for you, is important. For most people, it's a comfortable, happy retirement, and to get there, you have to understand your journey, plan your path, take the right roads and, above all, correct when you start to get off course.

There's another thing that you get to do on this journey, if you do it the *Every Dime, Every Day* way: you discover new routes and adventures that you never thought possible. I know that the receipt-keeping and the logbook, the 10/20/70 budget and the careful economizing to save even more seed money can all feel like you're climbing a huge mountain. But one day, you'll reach a certain level—like maybe when you achieve your first long-term goal or write a check for your own home rather than take out a mortgage—and you'll be at the top of that mountain. For the first time, you'll be able to see from one peak to the next. You'll be able to see what's truly possible in a way you never would have known if you had stayed stuck in those valleys.

Before Moving On
to the Next Chapter:

Use the descriptions in this chapter to determine what stage of your financial life you're in.

Go through the questions for your financial stage of life and consider each.

Make an action plan of the items you need to address for each question.

Begin addressing each action item and continue until you've addressed them all.

Chapter 12:

RISKS TO YOUR RETIREMENT

How you invest during retirement is as critical as how you invest in preparing for retirement. ... You can't rely on someone else coming up with the cash you'll need once you stop working.

~ Daniel R. Solin

Y ou may have heard about the "good old days" of retirement. Those were the days of pensions, and they had some benefits, to be sure. In those days, a person exchanged a lifetime of loyalty to one company for a pension that would keep that person comfortable for the rest of his or her life. In those days, the responsibility for retirement planning was entirely put on the employer. Today, that burden lies squarely on your own shoulders. That's a pretty enormous and daunting thing, when you think about it, but it comes with some benefits too. Along with all the responsibility comes another thing: control.

BUILDING AND PROTECTING YOUR DREAM RETIREMENT

Pensions, which our great-grandparents, grandparents, and maybe even parents depended on for retirement, are disappearing. Soon they'll likely be a distant memory. Today, no one is squirreling away savings for you during your working years. If you are going to have a comfortable income in retirement, or be able to retire *at all*, it's all on you.

One of the key building blocks of retirement for traditional employees is the employer-sponsored plan, such as the 401(k), 403(b), 457, or TSP account, just to name a few. In many cases, you'll get matching contributions from your employer (who is also making matching Social Security contributions on your behalf), but in order to get those matches, you have to contribute as well. In most cases, you have to meet a threshold contribution in order to receive the match, and you're still responsible for making decisions about how that money is invested. If you're self-employed, you're totally on your own.

Okay, you get it, right? Retirement planning is a solo mission these days. But there's good news too. First, it doesn't have to be—and shouldn't be—done totally on your own. More than ever, you need the guidance of a financial professional who has helped other retirees navigate these roads. When you find the right professional, you'll still get to be in charge of where you go.

In the pension days, you *did* get a regular check in the mail, it's true. That's because your employer took a little bit of money each year or month out of the salary you would have gotten, and that employer saved and invested that money. When you were ready to collect your pension, your employer paid it out of those investments. They decided how to create the income and how much income you'd receive.

Guess what? You're going to do the same thing today. Except today you get to decide how much to save. *You* choose where and how to invest. And *you* are in charge of how much income you'd like to create for retirement.

So, yes, we won't pretend this is not a BIG thing you have to do. It is. You have to save an enormous amount of money. You have to make some tricky, strategic decisions about how to handle that money, how to invest it so that it can grow, and how to set it up so that it can produce income in your retirement. And you have to know how to navigate all of the retirement pitfalls that lie in your path.

That's what we're going to discuss in this chapter: the pitfalls. No matter your age right now, you need to grasp these potential pitfalls right away because they're just that: potential. If you know what they are and how to avoid them, you can lay a smooth path for retirement that sidesteps every single one.

THE FIVE MAJOR PITFALLS OF A HAPPY RETIREMENT

Longevity. In the 1930s, people living to age 65 could expect to live another 13 years on average into retirement.[9] Today, people are living longer. Today's 65-year-olds can expect to live on average 20 years into retirement, but a significant number will live much longer: one out of four retirees will live into their 90s.[10] You could plan for 20 years of retirement income, but what if you are one of the lucky many who live 30 years or even longer into retirement? Running out of money at any time is a bad idea, but doing so at a time when you can't or shouldn't be returning to work is unacceptable.

Inflation. Along with living longer comes the risk of inflation. Inflation sounds like something getting bigger, but actually, it means that every dollar you have is worth less. It's a loss of spending power over time. For example, take something simple: a dozen eggs. Let's say you retired in May of 1985. You'd have paid $0.75 for your dozen eggs. If you lived 30 years into retirement, and you still wanted to make some breakfast, you would have needed more than double the money. You would need $1.96 for those same dozen eggs. That was the cheapest eggs were all year in 2015, by the way. They rose to

9   https://www.ssa.gov/history/lifeexpect.html
10   https://www.ssa.gov/planners/lifeexpectancy.html

almost $3 a dozen in late summer![11] The point is this: not only do you need to save enough money to pay your living expenses immediately after retirement, but you also have to include a plan to grow your assets, since inflation will mean you need more money to pay for the same expenses in the future.

Market volatility. The old stock market strategy used to be "buy and hold." That was it. You'd invest, hang on to your holdings for a few decades, and in the end, you'd have made a sizeable amount of money. But the market has changed. One big reason for that change is technology. Any kind of event, political, social, or business-related, can cause the delicate market to take a tumble or maybe even a terrifying crash. There was a time when those events took time to filter through, but today, with the Internet, we all have instant access to every event around the globe within seconds. The sharp highs and lows of the stock market in recent years are proof that volatility is here to stay, and investors need to be prepared with a new kind of strategy to counter that volatility. Retirees, who are counting on their investments for their everyday income, face the greatest risk when they don't have a plan to protect their assets. That plan is called *tactical management*, an investment strategy that allows your investments to be managed, changed, and adjusted all the time and immediately based on stock market shifts.

Healthcare. All that longevity means more time to do the things you've always dreamed of during retirement, but living longer also means that you're likely to need more healthcare as you age, and you'll need to pay that cost for years to come. If you're assuming, as so many people do, that Medicare will cover most of your healthcare costs, it's time to take a second look. Even taking Medicare into account, chances are very good that your out-of-pocket share of healthcare costs in retirement could eat up as much as (or more than) two-thirds of your lifetime Social Security benefit.[12] Remember, while many people do not pay any premium for Medicare Part A (hospital coverage), you will pay premiums for Part B, regular medical coverage, as well as deductibles and coinsurance.

---

11   https://data.bls.gov/pdq/SurveyOutputServlet
12   https://www.hvsfinancial.com/PublicFiles/Data_Release.pdf

What's more, *you* want to be in control of your healthcare, not give that control to some government agency. What if you needed a particular medicine to combat an illness or condition, but it wasn't something Medicare would approve? Would you want to be forced to go without it?

The key to all of this, once again, is saving. These costs sound prohibitive, and they can be, but only if you don't start saving for them early. Even if you have waited, there are savings strategies, such as a tax-free Health Savings Account, that could help you pay your healthcare costs without breaking the bank or sinking your retirement ship.

Long-term care. Because you're likely to live longer, you're also more likely than your predecessors to need long-term care. Long-term care is a term you'll hear a lot as you plan for your retirement, so let's take a minute to talk about what it is and what it is not.

Long-term care is a spectrum of services ranging from an aide who helps with tasks like house cleaning, cooking, grocery shopping, etc. all the way to 24-hour, in-facility medical care. Not only can these services be pricey, but they're also increasing rapidly. One month in an assisted living facility can cost an average of $3,628 per month, but if you retired today at age 65, you wouldn't likely need long-term care for 10 years or more. In 10 years, when you're 75, that same service will cost an estimated $4,876, and when you're 80, and much more likely to need assisted living or some other long-term care, it will cost an estimated $5,652.[13]

That's an increase of 34 percent in 10 years and 56 percent in 15 years. To put that in perspective, consider that Social Security provides a Cost of Living Adjustment (COLA) each year based on the Bureau of Labor Statistics' Consumer Price Index. The Social Security COLA was 0.3 percent. Over the past 10 years, the average COLA (which is zero in some years), has been 0.85 percent. So, over those 10 years, if you depended just on Social Security, you'd have received something in the neighborhood of an 8.5 percent increase in income, and you'd be facing more than 30 percent in long-term care cost increases.

---

13   https://www.genworth.com/about-us/industry-expertise/cost-of-care.html

Long-term care isn't the only cost that can increase faster than inflation. Other crucial expenses such as regular healthcare, heating, fuel, and even food can easily outpace inflation.

For all of these reasons, you need a retirement plan that is continuously growing yet not exposed to an undue amount of risk. Having a specific plan to pay for potential long-term care costs is one way to reduce risk. Long-term care insurance policies were once the standard way of planning for this cost, but these policies are growing harder to find and even harder to pay for. Typically, you have to plan early to get this kind of policy. Wait too long, and you won't be approved. Other options include hybrid programs that combine long-term care coverage with an insurance or annuity product. Usually these programs promise to pay out a certain monthly amount if long-term care is required, or they pay a death benefit to heirs if you never use the long-term care benefit.

FIND YOUR FOCUS

Retirement means a lot of amazing things (if you plan for it), but it also means that you are going to be unemployed for 20 or 30 years. Do you believe you can be both unemployed and living the best years of your life? You can, but it requires a lot of planning. It requires a tactical strategy, one that is laid out with the help of a retirement planning expert.

The first step when designing any great plan is finding focus. Time and time again, when I do interviews with potential new clients and we go through the fact finder together, I discover that most of the successful stories come down to people who live well within their means and automatically saved money for their later years. Many of those people didn't have specific retirement goals early on. They simply focused on saving. They built their savings to one level and then moved on to the next, working on saving and investing in stages. They kept their eyes on the prize—the long-term goal of building a nest egg—and that is what made all the difference.

Before Moving on
to the Next Chapter:

Zero in on saving. *Every Dime, Every Day* is the plan that will help you achieve that focus and jumpstart your savings, and that is a step you cannot skip. If you have not gotten your savings up to the 10 percent required in the 10/20/70 plan, make that your focus now. If you have, go through your logbook and find ways you can increase those savings. Increasing your savings by even a few percentage points now will make an exponential difference in your retirement income.

Chapter 13:

RETIRE ON YOUR TERMS

We have a retirement crisis in America today not from
a lack of money, but from a lack of vision.

~ Dave Ramsey

Anumber of years ago, I was speaking at a function for financial advisors, and I invited an advisor friend to join us. That day must have made an impression on him because he decided to make some changes to his finances. You see, he was making good money, and he could easily have gone on to live a high lifestyle, spending all that he was making. Instead, he took note of the *Every Dime, Every Day* plan and started to apply it to his own life. At the time, he just thought it was a good idea. As a financial advisor, he wanted to be able to help his own clients achieve financial independence, and so he felt he should set a good example. But too soon, he had an altogether different reason to be grateful for the changes he had made.

See, it wasn't long before he was able to amass some significant savings and investments. He and his wife were planning an early retirement, and they got one, but for all the wrong reasons. Before they could ever get to that retirement, his wife became very sick. She might have months left, or she might have a few years; the doctors just couldn't say. So, my friend took advantage of that financial independence he had worked so hard to build, and he took a temporary retirement. It turned out they had five years together, and those were years that they were actually able to be *together*, thanks to the fact that he had taken control of his finances.

PART ONE: PRESERVING YOUR ASSETS

You never know what might be in front of you: it could be big waves or smooth sailing, opportunities or a sea of troubles. Regardless, you want to be—and you can be—prepared. Having the financial independence to retire on your own terms, whatever they might be, is the exact kind of power that EDED will give you.

In the last chapter, we discussed some of the risks that every retiree faces and the secret to laying a strong retirement foundation regardless of the risks: *saving more.* Remember, no matter what financial stage of life you're in, it's never too late to get control of your spending, figure out your finances, and start living on a budget that includes significant saving.

Saving, however, is just the first step. In the Accumulation phase, you focus on saving and planting those savings in the richest soil possible so that they can grow long and strong over the next few decades. By doing that, you're laying the groundwork for financial independence, and the better your groundwork, the more options you're going to have later. But what happens as you approach retirement?

STEER YOUR OWN SHIP

As you get closer to your retirement day, you begin to enter into the Preservation stage. This is the part of your financial life where you want to start taking stock of what you have so that you can best position your assets for your future. To use a nautical metaphor, you might think of retirement as a sea voyage, and the Preservation stage is when you're loading up your ship in preparation for the day you sail away from port. Everything you have stockpiled needs to be preserved: protected from moisture, bad weather, and big waves. It's time to think about how best to position your assets where they can generate income for you without being exposed to quite so much volatility and risk.

During the Accumulation phase, the vast majority of people have their retirement savings on autopilot: they have X amount of dollars taken out of each paycheck and put directly into a 401(k), 403(b), 457 plan, Thrift Savings Plans (TSA), TIAA-CREF, or any other employer-sponsored retirement plan. Hopefully, the company's matching contribution goes in there as well. Generally speaking, these accounts rely on **passive investment strategies**, namely buy and hold. A fund manager or broker buys stocks and bonds and holds them for a long time period, regardless of market highs and lows, and because the investors aren't taking anything out of these accounts, everything generally grows and works out just fine.

All of that, however, is about to change.

CRITICAL CHANGES AHEAD

Once you pull up the anchor that is your paycheck and sail off into the wild blue yonder, taking a hit by the big waves suddenly starts to matter. When you're taking money out of your savings account for income to live on, you can't afford any additional leaks in your boat. This is where **tactical management strategies** allow you to weather the losses without sinking the ship. An actively managed portfolio that benefits from a tactical strategy is one where your advisor buys or sells investments based on market conditions. If you're working with an investment adviser representative, they will have the ability to manage your portfolio for growth while also seeking to preserve a portion of your portfolio for income distribution. This way, no matter the weather, your income might be preserved.

As you enter into the Preservation stage, you have some decisions to make. The worst thing you can do is to not make any decisions at all. Too many people get to the end of their Accumulation years and leave their retirement savings on autopilot because it's easy and comfortable. They know that a passive investment strategy works, and so they retire with no coordinated plan. They think, *It's worked pretty well for me so far. Why would I change now?*

You need to make a change because the job of your portfolio is about to change. Once you stop working, your portfolio is going to be the one generating the paycheck, so you want to do everything you can to position this money in the best way possible. And you want to do this as you near retirement, before market waves, tax inefficiencies, long-term care, and uncoordinated decisions put too many holes in your retirement ship. Because here's the thing: you really are on your own. Most people don't have the iron-clad stability of a regular pension. You can try to get one using one of the solutions we talked about earlier, in Chapter 9, and you can choose to work with a fiduciary professional who will go over your portfolio to make sure everything is shipshape. Or, you can head out into the deep water alone and hope there's no sharks or waves or storms for the next 20 to 30 years.

I don't mean to make it sound all doom and gloom. There will be plenty of gorgeous sunsets and bright shining waters as well. The point here is this: *you're not just in charge of doing all the saving, you're also responsible for protecting those savings.*

One of the most responsible things you can do is to find an advisor who can help you navigate the changes ahead. As you close in on retirement, in your 50s and 60s, you need an advisor who specializes not in accumulation, but in retirement planning, which involves first preserving your assets and second, creating a retirement income plan. It's certainly possible that your financial professional has expertise in both accumulation and preservation, passive strategies and tactical ones, but this isn't an area where you want to take any chances. Now is the time to ask questions and, if necessary, find a financial professional who is a better fit for your changing needs.

QUESTIONS TO ASK A POTENTIAL RETIREMENT PLANNING PROFESSIONAL:

Are you a fiduciary?

As we discussed in Chapter 8: Finding the Right Financial Professional, "fiduciary responsibility" is a phrase you want attached to any financial professional you choose to help plan your retirement. Financial professionals who are held to a fiduciary standard, often referred to as being a fiduciary, are legally bound to offer you advice that puts your interest ahead of their own. Fiduciaries cannot recommend a high-commission product, for example, that is simply suitable for you, but not in your best interest.

How do you help your clients transition from the Accumulation stage into Preservation and then retirement (Distribution)? If your potential advisor has no plans to change your risk exposure or your investments at all, that's a red flag. What you're looking for here is an advisor who:

Understands that your circumstances are changing and your investments must be adjusted accordingly.

Has a method for helping you create a retirement and income plan based on your specific goals and circumstances.

No cookie-cutter plans for you! Be wary of any financial professional who puts you in one financial vehicle —such as a variable annuity— to solve all of your retirement planning needs. These types of one-size-fits-all planning solutions might not only be expensive, but dangerous to the long-term stability of your portfolio.

What training/certifications or experience do you have specifically in retirement planning?

There are a lot of different certifications in the financial planning world, and you can decide which ones are important to you. But I would suggest that experience and references are the most important ways you can judge whether a financial professional is right for you. Ask your financial professional about his or her experience with retirement planning, and ask for references from clients whose situations are similar to yours. This will help you know if the financial professional truly understands your retirement goals, and it will give you a sense of what it would be like to work with that advisor.

What investment management style do you use?

This is a complex topic. We talked earlier about passive management styles (sometimes called the passive/buy-and-hold strategy) and the tactical style, which is sometimes called an active management strategy. There is another **active investment strategy** known as day trading, but be aware that this is not the same thing as a tactical strategy. Day trading is an active investment strategy where a manager or broker frequently buys stocks and usually holds them for a day or less. This type of strategy is not only inefficient from a tax standpoint, it also poses greater risk to the investor. It does, however, have the ability to outperform the benchmark index, unlike the passive strategies that, generally speaking, are unlikely to outperform benchmark indices.

It's also worth noting that the individual investor trying to figure out a strategy on their own isn't likely to fair well. According to Dalbar's 2016 Quantitative Analysis of Investor Behavior, the average equity mutual fund investor underperformed the S&P 500 by a margin of 3.66 percent.[14]

---

14 http://www.northstarfinancial.com/files/6314/6523/9571/2016_DALBAR_Advisor_Edition.pdf

During retirement, you want an investment strategy that meets your risk tolerance, comfort level, and financial goals. A tactical management style combines the best of both passive and active strategies. It is reactive to changes in the market, attempts to limit market risk, and has the ability to achieve greater returns.

How and how often do you communicate with your clients?

Some advisors have a set communication plan with clients, such as quarterly or annual meetings, sending monthly or quarterly email updates, and so on. Other advisors are willing to customize their communication to your preference. Either way, the timing and content of communication need to meet your needs and comfort level. You should never, ever be left wondering what's happening with your nest egg, and you should always have a way to contact your advisor immediately with concerns or questions.

What is your fee structure?

Look for an advisor who charges a flat fee, usually a percentage of your portfolio. This puts you on the same team: when you earn, your advisor earns.

KNOW WHAT YOU WANT

Once you have the financial professional you want, you can start discussing a plan that will help you have *the retirement you want*. That's what this is all about.

Earlier, I mentioned that you don't want a cookie-cutter retirement plan. That's because every person is unique—your financial circumstances, family situation, goals for retirement, and so on. Why would you settle for anything less than a retirement plan that is customized to your exact specifications?

But if you want to get a plan that is customized to you, first you have to know exactly what it is you want. Here are some things to consider:

If you knew you could spend your retirement doing anything you wanted, without risk, what would you do?

If you only had one year of retirement to live, what five things would you want to accomplish?

Who do you want to spend your retirement with?

Where do you want to spend your retirement?

When you do you want to stop working?

What does your logbook tell you about the minimum amount of income you need to maintain your life now, pre-retirement?

PART TWO: CREATING A RETIREMENT INCOME PLAN

During your working years, income comes in the form of a paycheck. You work. You get paid. You get income. During retirement, you will generate your income from all the saving you did while you were working. Once you start doing that, you've entered into the Distribution stage of your financial journey.

FILE FOR YOUR SOCIAL SECURITY BENEFIT

For most people, the foundation of retirement income is Social Security. You've been paying into Social Security your entire working life; now is when that pays off. But you should know that there are a lot of misconceptions about Social Security. For example, many people believe that the amount they will receive from Social Security is a fixed number based solely on their pre-retirement salary. In reality, the amount of your Social Security check is affected by a lot of factors, in particular, the age at which you decide to start collecting Social Security. As a retiree, you are eligible to begin collecting as early as 62, but if you are able to wait to collect, you could significantly increase each Social Security check. That's because your Social Security benefit continues to increase until age 70, when it reaches its highest possible amount.

For some people, waiting until age 70 to collect Social Security is a good strategy to optimize reliable income. Married couples in particular will want to consider this when planning their income, because when one spouse passes away, the other spouse is eligible for the larger of the two Social Security benefits. Other things to consider are your financial situation, your health, other income sources, and your retirement goals.

If you've made the choice to work with an investment adviser representative, he or she will be able to run a comprehensive Social Security planning strategy report to help you determine the best time to file. If you're not working with an advisor who can get this report for you, consider getting a second opinion from someone who can. Your monthly Social Security check is your income foundation. The more dollars you get from this important lifetime benefit, the fewer dollars you'll need to fill your income gap.

CALCULATE YOUR INCOME GAP

Once your Social Security benefit is in place, the next step is to calculate how much more income you'll need each month. Luckily, you've got your logbook to tell you.

Subtract the amount you'll receive from Social Security from the total income you need each month. The difference is called your "**income gap**." You'll use your assets—savings, 401(k), IRA, etc.—to generate the income that fills that gap. There are lots of different ways to do that; some options come with more risk while others offer a bit more safety. The right retirement plan will generate the income you need while also giving you peace of mind. You absolutely don't want to spend your retirement watching the stock market and worrying that your nest egg could crack wide open with the next economic downturn.

DO SOMETHING THAT MAKES YOU HAPPY

Being financially independent will solve a lot of problems and ease a lot of worries, but it isn't the only ingredient in a happy retirement. As you make all of these strategic plans for your retirement income, don't forget to spend some time considering all the other plans you should be making. After all, this is a time when you should be doing all of the things that your working life schedule never allowed. For example,

Get active. Even if you've never had time for a serious fitness habit, now is a great time to make the decision to get active. The more active you are in retirement, the healthier you'll be. What's the use in saving all this money if you don't stay healthy enough to enjoy it?

Keep a calendar. It's easy to let the days slip by in retirement, so make

DO I HAVE TO MAINTAIN A LOGBOOK DURING RETIREMENT?

The number one fear of most retirees today is running out of money. Not only are we living longer than we used to, but we've also entered into a global economy. The stock market is more volatile and things can change overnight based on news from other parts of the world. How can you relax with any kind of certainty during your golden years during such uncertain times?

The answer is your logbook. Even during retirement it's important to keep track of where your money is going, both in and out. If you've got a good plan, you'll have both interest-bearing accounts and lifetime benefit checks. Doing your record keeping will not only help you stay within your budget, it will give you peace of mind as well. You'll be able to see that, yes, your spending is on track, and yes, even though the market just took a hit, your retirement is still on course. The logbook is a habit that will soon become second nature. Most people find it to be such a powerful tool, they don't want to stop doing it because they see and enjoy such positive results.

some plans. Dream big—plan those trips you always wanted to take— and keep it simple. Create a schedule that gets you walking at the park or hiking some nearby trails. Talk to your financial professional about planning ahead for those big dreams so you can make them happen within budget.

Stay on budget. Yes, I'm repeating myself. But this is the key to a happy retirement. It's not about being rich. It's about knowing that when your heating bill arrives, you can pay it. It's about staying on the EDED plan, even during retirement, so that you can take all your money worries off the table. A worry-free retirement is a happy retirement.

Before Moving on to the Next Chapter:

Using your logbook, make a list of all of your current expenses.

Compare those expenses to the vision you have created for your retirement. Which expenses will increase, which will stay the same, and which will decrease?

Create an estimated retirement budget based on your findings. Keep it to the 10/20/70 plan! Saving in retirement is just as important. It will help you feel secure, regardless of how many happy retirement years are ahead, and it will help you cover costs, such as healthcare, that might increase. It can also help you save for those big dreams, such as travel, buying the cabin on the lake you've always wanted, or maybe taking your grandkids to Disneyworld.

If you are in or nearing the Preservation or Distribution stages, it's time to choose your retirement specialist and get started on your income plan! You will work with your financial professional to create a budget that takes into account Social Security and other income sources, using your assets to generate the additional income you require.

Chapter 14:

Find Your Financial Common Sense

If you want something you have never had, you must be willing to do something you have never done.

~ Thomas Jefferson

Good habits are hard to make and they're also hard to maintain. We all know this from our New Year's resolutions. We get all excited about making big changes in our lives, and sometimes we're successful, and then ... we get tired. We get good behavior fatigue. At those times, we all need a little inspiration to stay dedicated. That's what this chapter is all about.

HOW TO USE THIS CHAPTER

Read this chapter straight through if the mood strikes you. Or, go directly to the topic you're struggling with today and dig in to the bits of wisdom that you need right now. Or, do both. This chapter is your place to go when you need something extra to keep going.

DEBT

Avoid debt at all costs unless you're taking on a debt to attain an asset that will increase your income. Otherwise, debt is cancer.

A borrower is a slave to the lender in all cases.

Don't hide from your debt. If you can't make all your minimum payments, call the creditors and renegotiate some of the terms of the payments. Creditors prefer to get paid, and often they will work with you to lower interest rates or work out a payment structure that works with your budget. It's always better to pay a little on everything than to pay some bills one month and leave others out.

If you have to have credit cards that you won't be able to pay off each month, shop for the lowest interest rate.

Treat debt like a game with the Debt Knockout method. The objective of the game is to knock out the smallest balance first by throwing the largest ball you can (payment) directly at it. Once you eliminate that balance—with a giant feeling of satisfaction—cross it off and move to the next smallest balance.

Use visuals to stay motivated. Keep lists of everything and mark your progress. Money can be so abstract. That's why it's so easy to hide from our money problems until we get deep into trouble. But when you have a visual, you can see your progress. You can watch your game plan playing out and be reminded that you *do* have the power to control your finances.

Avoid consolidating loans. This is presented as a way to save money, but too often when payments are reduced, the money that would have been spent toward paying down debt just gets spent on lifestyle, not saved. For example, let's say you have $3,000 in monthly debt payments, but you only have $2,500 to spend on them. You consolidate, and now your debt payment totals $1,500. What do you do with the $1,000 excess? It should go to paying off the loan as quickly as possible. But that's not what usually happens.

If there is no other way to make all of your debt payments without consolidating, and you simply must consolidate, make a commitment to yourself that you will not buy anything on credit again until you pay off the consolidated loan. If you need a credit card for things like online purchases, use a debit card that's directly linked to your bank account so that you can finance your purchases responsibly.

Anytime you finance anything, be sure there is no prepayment penalty.

Compound interest is a beautiful thing when it's working for you, as in an investment account, but it works against you just as much when it's applied to a debt, like your credit cards.

CARS

The ideal way to pay for a car is in one payment. Write a check. If you need to take a loan, you might consider whether you could make do with a less expensive car.

Buying a brand-new car is almost never a good idea. It will depreciate as much as 9 percent the moment you drive it off the lot and as much as 19 percent in the first year you own it.[15] Buy a car that is a few years old, and you can get the dependability you seek with a much smarter price tag.

Never finance a luxury (and this applies to more than cars). For example, if you're considering buying a car, but you need a 5-year loan to afford the payments, then you simply can't afford it.

Leasing is very rarely the best deal because of all the fine print such as penalties for going over a certain mileage or for ending the lease early. Only occasionally, leasing a car rather than buying it will pencil out,

---

15 https://www.edmunds.com/car-buying/how-fast-does-my-new-car-lose-value-infographic.html

often because of tax deductions, but check with your tax specialist to be sure.

Before you take a test drive, make the firm decision that you won't buy that day. Because most buying is impulsive, the salesperson's goal is to get you in that car, driving it, smelling its new car smell, and then signing those papers as soon as possible. (Believe me, I know.)

FAMILY FINANCES

The breadwinner(s) of a family should always control the checkbook. Whomever is bringing in the money should see where it is going. Seeing that savings are going up and debt is going away—that will keep the breadwinner motivated.

It's equally important that both spouses be involved in the finances. Everyone needs to be motivated to limit spending and increase savings, and you never want one spouse to have no investment in or knowledge of your financial situation.

HOW YOU THINK

Short-term thinkers end up broke. Always keep an eye on your long-term goals—five, 10, 15 years in the future—and measure the decisions you're making now by how they will affect those goals.

Make your goal-setting visual. Write it down. Draw a graph. Update it with your progress. You need something physical you can see and strive for.

Create a picture of where you want to be in 10 years. Write down a description. Draw a picture. Make a collage. Do whatever you need to do to make your long-term goals feel real to you.

INSURANCE

Continually reassess your insurance coverage to ensure you aren't paying too much for coverage you don't need.

If your car value is low, eliminate collision and keep liability.

The larger your net worth grows, the larger your deductibles should grow on your vehicles and property. This saves you a tremendous amount of money in premiums but still covers catastrophic events.

Check insurance rates before you buy a car. Even the color of a car can sometimes dramatically change the rates you'll pay.

MISTAKES YOU CAN AVOID

Living a consumptive lifestyle and spending compulsively might give you a few seconds of pleasure but will certainly cause a lifetime of regret.

Keeping up with the Joneses: if you're spending to maintain a certain appearance, stop. This is a big problem in America, trying to appear like you have a certain lifestyle when all you're actually doing is creating a life of anxiety and stress.

Don't spend because you feel guilty. Give the people you love more security and more of your time, not more stuff.

Never operate without a plan. You can—and should—adjust your goals and your plan regularly, but if you are operating without an idea of what your life is about and what you want to achieve, you'll never be able to live a life you love.

Stop focusing on possessions and put your focus on savings instead. Think: I could buy any car I want, but what feels even better is knowing that I could do that, but choose instead to drive a reasonable car while keeping my savings balance high.

Don't give personal loans. When you have accumulated sizeable assets, this could become a question, but protect your relationships and say no. Psychologically, the borrower becomes a slave to the lender, no matter how good your intentions. Never sacrifice your relationships over money.

MORTGAGES

What's the best length for a mortgage? If you need a mortgage, try to buy a house that you can afford if your mortgage is 15 years. If you're finding 30-year rates that are significantly less, making it possible to lock it in at less than 4 percent, you could consider that. Then pay additional principal payments, allowing you to pay it off in 15 years or less.

Never just meet with one banker when looking for a mortgage. Use competition to get yourself the best deal possible. And remember, you might trust your local bank that you've been with for years, but they aren't always able to give the best deals.

Online mortgage rates and quotes can help guide you so that you can shop for the best deals.

Look at a mortgage amortization calculator, which will show you how much of each payment goes toward your principal and how much goes to interest. If you can pay next month's principal payment as well as this month's, you'll pay off the house 10 years sooner.

Also, consider making mortgage payments every two weeks: it could cut six years off your mortgage term.

Is there a prepayment penalty on the mortgage you're considering? Many people sign their mortgage papers without ever realizing that the prepayment penalty is there. It *is* negotiable, so pay attention.

The payments you'll make on a mortgage over 15 years will be 16 percent higher than the payments on a 30-year mortgage. *But* after 10 years, you've paid off 45 percent with the 15-year mortgage, and with the 30-year loan, you've only paid off 5 percent in 10 years. Finance charges add an enormous amount to the bottom line on longer loans.

Never refinance without doing all the math. Many people don't consider all the actual costs—closing costs, fees, etc.—which can undercut all of the benefit of refinancing. For example, if it will cost $5,000 total to refinance, and your refinanced mortgage will save you $300 a month, it will take 17 payments just to break even. You won't be saving any money until a year and a half after you refinance.

Also, take into account the possibility of selling. If there's any chance you might sell in a year or two, it makes no sense to pay the costs of refinancing.

Beware of home equity loans: you're giving up the asset of equity in your home and most of these loans are variable rate, so you have no control over interest rate changes. You're stuck paying whatever the interest rate becomes.

ORGANIZATION

Set up an office in your home. Carve out a section, a room, any space that you can dedicate to your financial work. Remember, you're running your home like a business, and you're the CEO. You deserve an office where you can organize all of the tools you need to do that successfully.

Controlling your household financially and physically go hand in hand, so when you're cleaning up your finances, clear out the clutter too. Both are about control and discipline. Clear the decks.

Are you hanging on to things because you believe you'll need them later and won't be able to afford them? Let go of that story. It's contrary to everything you're doing. Let go of the story *and* all the stuff you don't need right now.

Go to the garage, clear the clutter from your house, sell it all, and put it toward your debt or savings.

Pay attention to what works for you and use that. My most effective, efficient time is the day before I go on vacation. I know I will be able to enjoy my vacation more and focus when I return home only if I get my desk and papers cleared and organized and my work done.

SAVING

You might think there is no extra money you could be saving, but when you start logging your monthly expenses, most people can find ways to adjust or eliminate expenses so that more money can be put toward debt or savings.

Set a liquid emergency savings goal as a buffer. This is a number that you will never let your savings account dip below. How much of a buffer will make you sleep well at night? $10,000? $50,000? It might sound impossible now, but we did it. Our absolute top savings goal used to be $100,000 and now, we worry when we dip below that!

No matter your financial situation, saving at least 10 percent of your earnings is a must. It teaches you discipline and motivates you.

If you have negative cash flow—more bills than income—and saving seems impossible, that means you can't afford the lifestyle you're living.

Don't be ashamed of saving money. My family still uses coupons. We take advantage of every opportunity to keep more of the money we work hard to earn.

Someone who saves $10 a week over 40 years, with compounding interest, can have a net worth of over $1.2 million. You can accomplish that just by cutting out a couple of trips per week to Starbucks. But staying poor is just as subtle. If you spend an extra $10 per week, it eats away at your assets just as significantly over time.

SPENDING

Two things determine what you do with your money: your commitments and your priorities. Commitments are easily identified: your kids, your mortgage and so on. But priorities are harder to nail down. People talk a lot about what they believe about money, but if you want to know what their priorities truly are, look at what they spend their money on. Those are their true priorities.

Grocery shop after you eat, when you're not hungry, and always make a list and buy only what is on your list. Never forget that marketing drives grocery store setups: they're designed to play to your impulses.

Never make a major purchase like a car or house without sleeping on it. This will give you some space to consider carefully and be sure you're not making an emotional decision. Emotion drives a lot of unnecessary spending. Every purchase should make sense and not just give you a momentary good feeling.

Never hesitate to make an investment in yourself. If there's a course you can take that will make your earnings potential better, do it.

A lot of people want a million-dollar lifestyle, but they have a $50 library. That doesn't work.

You can't spend indiscriminately and expect to be financially successful. Even if you manage to earn a lot of money, it won't help because if you can't manage small amounts of money, you won't be able to handle large ones. Just look at lottery winners: nearly a third of them end up declaring bankruptcy.[16]

Always negotiate. Virtually everything is negotiable. And pay with cash: you'll increase your ability to negotiate remarkably.

Another reason to use cash: people spend significantly more when they use credit cards.[17]

---

16   http://fortune.com/2016/01/15/powerball-lottery-winners/

17   https://www.psychologytoday.com/blog/the-science-behind-behavior/201607/
does-it-matter-whether-you-pay-cash-or-credit-card

Always shop around. There are alternatives everywhere, whether you're shopping for cars, shoes, jewelry, or even insurance.

Use the Internet before making a big purchase. You can find out a lot about the best deals available and be better prepared to negotiate.

Use a purchasing sounding board. Often, clients will ask me for advice before making a big purchase, and this is a great idea. If you run your potential purchases through a third party who has no vested interest or emotion about the purchase, you'll make a wiser decision every time.

Taxes

Taxes are something many people try to ignore until they absolutely have to attend to them. Then, they do as little as possible and try to forget them again until the next year. Break that habit. Hire a CPA or tax professional. Keep your records current throughout the year. Take advantage of all of the deductions and tax laws that apply to you, and save yourself stress: be sure you know that every detail is on the up and up.

Many people get huge refunds from the IRS at tax time. If you are one of them, but you also have credit card or other debts, why not decrease your withholdings and keep some of that money for yourself? Instead of giving the government an interest-free loan, you could be paying it toward debt and saving yourself lots of unnecessary interest on your own debts.

Treat Your Personal Finances like a Business

Reconcile your checkbook/accounts within 24 hours of getting statements in the mail. Make it a habit. Check every charge for control purposes. You might be surprised at the mistakes you find.

Make yourself a financial statement each month: list everything you own, whether you have debt on it or not, and everything you owe.

Make a new balance sheet every month and at the end of each year. Pay attention to your profits (savings) and any losses (debts). If you're following EDED, you'll be seeing more and more profits every month, and you will be able to see your debts decreasing. That's progress you can see, and it will keep you motivated.

VALUE AND WORTH

Understand that when you're spending time on something, you're trading that time for money. People will frequently ask for favors, and it's fine to give favors. It's great. But be careful with them. You wouldn't let people steal your money, so why let them steal your time?

Always know your hourly rate, even if you aren't technically paid by the hour. It gives you a ruler to measure the worth of everything you do or buy. If you make $20 an hour, and you're considering buying a $5 coffee, take a moment and think: Would I be willing to work 15 minutes for this coffee? You probably wouldn't even want to *wait* 15 minutes for it.

WARRANTIES

Extended warranties on things like appliances, cars, etc. are not usually a good deal. Do careful research before you hand over a chunk of money that won't benefit you.

WHAT DO YOU DESERVE?

Don't fall into the trap of thinking, *I work hard so I deserve this fancy car or expensive vacation.* You deserve what you can afford. And you can save for what you truly deserve.

If you can't afford something, the word "deserve" doesn't come into the equation.

Also, don't be tempted to think, *I work hard, so my kids deserve this expensive thing.* Above all, your kids deserve a strong foundation for their financial future, and I don't mean an inheritance. They deserve to learn crucial skills like delayed gratification and self-discipline.

WHEN YOU'RE DISCOURAGED

Your head is out of the sand. Just by reading this book, you've taken a huge step: you're no longer hiding from your situation. Even if you've lost some ground, just figure out how to move forward again.

Never be embarrassed about taking steps back if necessary. The vast majority of people never realize when they're in a bad spot, when they're losing ground. So, be proud of yourself for realizing that.

It's always okay to regroup and reassess. In fact, the most successful people are constantly reassessing.

Doing more of something that doesn't work is never going to improve anything, no matter how good your intentions are.

Where do you want to be? Figure that out and write it down. Describe it in detail. Then get started on (or get back to) your plan on how to get there.

You are taking control of your finances, and that is an enormous accomplishment. Financial control is the link between dreaming of a better life and actually accomplishing one.

YOUR TRUE NET WORTH

Know the difference between an asset and a liability. The simple definitions: an asset is anything that you own the value on, and a liability is anything you owe money on.

Being brutally honest with yourself about the true value of your "assets" is the only way to start making progress. For example, you might consider your car an asset, but is it? Here's the best way to tell: if you had to sell it in 60 days, what can you really get for it? If you have a car loan for $20,000, and you can only sell the car for $21,000, then that "asset" is only worth $1,000.

Remember that every dollar you ever spend changes your net worth. That pastry you just bought lowered your net worth. But anything that grows in value, such as an investment, adds to your net worth.

SIDEBAR

Five Things You Can Do with Money (Besides Get More Stuff)

Declare war on debt. You've probably heard stories about people committing suicide when they lost everything in the Great Depression, but many people also became millionaires during that time. If you eliminate debt and save now, you'll be prepared to take advantage of opportunities even in hard times.

FIVE THINGS YOU CAN DO WITH MONEY (BESIDES GET MORE STUFF)

Declare war on debt. You've probably heard stories about people committing suicide when they lost everything in the Great Depression, but many people also became millionaires during that time. If you eliminate debt and save now, you'll be prepared to take advantage of opportunities even in hard times.

Pay your taxes. You may disagree with tax policy, and you wouldn't be alone, but in the end, you need to pay. Not being able to pay your taxes is a far more stressful situation.

Give. When you have saved well and increased your assets, you can be in a position to help causes that you believe in. Find some purpose that touches your heart and watch the enormous positive effect you can have thanks to your discipline and hard work.

Seed your future. Put your extra cash away and plant it somewhere it can grow for your future. Small sacrifices now will allow you to grow much greater freedom and happiness in your future.

Pay your bills. If you've ever been in a position of trying to choose which bills to pay, then you know the great relief and happiness that comes from having *enough*. If you can't pay all your bills, call your creditors. They will be willing to work with you.

Pay your taxes. You may disagree with tax policy, and you wouldn't be alone, but in the end, you need to pay. Not being able to pay your taxes is a far more stressful situation.

Give. When you have saved well and increased your assets, you can be in a position to help causes that you believe in. Find some purpose that touches your heart and watch the enormous positive effect you can have thanks to your discipline and hard work.

Seed your future. Put your extra cash away and plant it somewhere it can grow for your future. Small sacrifices now will allow you to grow much greater freedom and happiness in your future.

Pay your bills. If you've ever been in a position of trying to choose which bills to pay, then you know the great relief and happiness that comes from having *enough*. If you can't pay all your bills, call your creditors. They will be willing to work with you.

CHANGE YOUR BELIEFS

Discipline will change your financial situation and your life, but first you have to change your beliefs.

Almost invariably, the person with the least amount of money in a restaurant will order the most expensive thing. Often people act rich when they aren't, and just as often, those people never will be what they pretend. The behavior of most truly rich people might surprise you. Thomas Stanley famously researched the habits of millionaires and published several books, such as *The Millionaire Next Door* and *Stop Acting Rich ... and Start Living like a Real Millionaire*. He found that three times more millionaires live in homes valued at under $300,000 than in homes valued at over $1 million, and many more millionaires drive Toyotas than luxury cars.

Millionaires are everyday people who have uncommon ways of thinking about and dealing with money. There is no reason you can't be one of them. Don't resist making a permanent change that will positively change your life and deliver long-term gain.

The first belief change you need to make is this: believe in yourself. Stop blocking yourself with negative thoughts. Making yourself wealthy is not about anything other than discipline. Take it from multimillionaire investor Peter Shankman, who said, "It's amazing how much smarter everyone thinks you are once you have money. Two days after I sold my company, I got asked to speak at a conference I had been trying desperately to speak at for six years."

He was just as smart the day before he sold his company, but no one was taking his calls at that fancy conference. It's a good thing for him that he decided to believe in his own intelligence and push forward rather than wait for other people to treat him like they believed he was smart. Believe in yourself first. If you do that, everyone else will believe in you eventually.

With a determined belief in yourself, turn to discipline and start making the changes that will change your life. Keep your logbook. Maintain your budget. If you get off track, stop, take a moment to reassess, and get right back on.

Above all, keep your focus on your goals. You are making a big difference in your life.

Before Moving on to the Next Chapter:

Mark all of the tidbits in this chapter that you particularly want or need to work on. Come back to them whenever you need to find focus again.

Create a plan to help you stay committed to EDED. Write yourself notes and place them around the house or in your desk. Ask your spouse to remind you. The sacrifices you're making now are going to add up to extraordinary differences in your future life.

Chapter 15:
YOU WERE BORN TO SUCCEED

Always bear in mind that your own resolution to
succeed is more important than any other.

~ Abraham Lincoln

There is a dangerous belief out there, one that is threatening your dreams, your future success, and your happiness: it's the rumor that the only real way to get ahead financially is to inherit some money. Let's get this straight right now: that is not true. Not even the tiniest bit true. How do I know? That's the story I was told growing up. *Don't get too big for your britches, kid. You're stuck right here in the circumstances where you were born. Don't feel bad, though. We're all stuck. You're no different. The deck is just stacked for the rich people, and that's how it is.*

This is a story that people tell themselves to feel better about their circumstances. I'm not saying they're lying. They believe it, and they have good reason. The kind of change that is required to reverse bad money habits is very difficult. That's why I've broken the *Every Dime, Every Day* process into small, manageable steps. Doing them all at

147

once, or trying to conquer every one of your goals at once, is like trying to leap over a mountain. You don't leap mountains. You climb them one step at a time, usually with gear and a team of people and sometimes even oxygen. But mountains can be climbed, if you do it one step at a time, and you can achieve financial independence too.

GET STUBBORN

As we all go through life, things like occupations, experiences, and relationships will come and go. It's hard to see while it's happening, but all of those things combine and build to bring you to the point where you are today. They aren't all necessarily good or happy experiences, either. I look back on all of the struggles and disappointments of my young life, all the sweat and hard work I put into every job and project, only to come out with nothing to show for them in the end.

For a while I believed the story I had been told growing up, that this was just how life was for people like me. And then I simply decided I didn't want to believe that anymore. I decided I would refuse to believe it. That was when I was able to start making changes.

MORE OPPORTUNITY THAN YOU EVER IMAGINED

In one of my favorite books, *The 7 Habits of Highly Successful People*, author Stephen R. Covey explains that most people have a deeply ingrained Scarcity Mentality. This means that they see the world as having only so much opportunity, like all of the success and happiness is just one big pie, and since they can see that other people have big slices of that pie, there's not going to be any left for them.

Growing up, that was all I ever knew. I remember when I was moving back to Maine from Florida at age 19, and my Uncle Benny—my second-father/big-brother hero—flew down to make the drive with me. It was a 1,500-mile drive, and we drove straight through, taking turns, so that we wouldn't have to stop and pay for a hotel. As we passed the interstate signs for Washington, D.C., I will never forget what Benny said. He looked at me and said, "Hey maybe we should stop in D.C. We'll never have this chance again, and wouldn't it be interesting to walk around and see all the things there?"

At that moment, I saw exactly how different our outlooks on life were. My instant reaction was, *How is it possible that we could never have this chance again?* I was so shocked that he would even consider that he might never have the chance to travel, to D.C. or anywhere else. If it was something he wanted to do, why wouldn't he just make it happen?

We didn't stop in the end. Benny didn't really care that much about it, or at least he didn't seem to. But he never did go back, either. These days, when I'm on a trip, either for work or with my family, I usually give Uncle Benny a call. I want him to remember that trip, how it was both of us driving in that car from Florida to Maine, how he thought neither of us had the slightest chance of traveling, but now I travel whenever I want.

My intent isn't to make him feel bad. I want him to see that if I can do it, so can he. It's not too late for him to travel. It's not too late for you. It's never too late to make your dreams come true. Now is the time to start seeing the Abundance in the world.

HOW TO TEACH YOURSELF TO SEE ABUNDANCE

Is it even possible to stop seeing life as a big pie, most of which is already being enjoyed by other people? It is possible, and even more importantly, it's necessary. If you continue looking at life as though most of the good parts are already taken, reserved for someone else, why would you even bother doing the hard work that's required to succeed, financially or otherwise?

If you have the Scarcity Mentality, you already know it. Even if you don't admit it out loud, you probably worry when others have big successes. You're happy for them, but something inside you feels like success for others means less success for yourself. But I promise you, this is a mentality you learned, not one you were born with or even one you observed to be true. Just try this exercise:

Write down a list of all of your closest associates, the people you spend most of your time with. Being honest (this isn't something you ever need to show to anyone!), consider whether each of those people has a mentality of Scarcity or Abundance.

Spend more time in Abundance. If there are people on your list who see a world full of possibilities, who are generous in spirit and have a joy you don't experience in the others, those are the people you want to spend more time with. If you don't have any people in your life who fit that description, it's time to find some.

Look for people—friends or mentors—who can help foster your sense of Abundance. Once you start paying attention to this, chances are very good that you'll realize they're all around.

Find Abundance in books. You can always bolster the amount of Abundance in your life by reading. Biographies and memoirs are excellent sources of inspiration. There are endless examples of people who didn't start out with any advantages and yet succeeded against all odds.

Walt Disney had a less-than-idyllic childhood, and his start in the business world was no more auspicious. He was even fired from a newspaper once for "lacking creativity."

Candymaker Milton Hershey became one of America's most legendary businessmen, but he was born on a small farm, didn't finish school, and started several ventures that failed before he discovered the delicious power of caramel and then figured out a way to mass-produce milk chocolate.

Cosmetics mogul Mary Kay Ash grew up caring for her ill father while her mother worked long days in a restaurant to support the family. She later excelled at her sales job, despite suffering from rheumatoid arthritis, but when she was passed over for a promotion, she'd had enough. She took a small investment and started Mary Kay Cosmetics at age 45. Mary Kay Cosmetics today sells nearly $3 billion annually, and the Mary Kay Foundation raises millions of dollars each year for causes like cancer, domestic violence, and human trafficking.

The examples above are all of average people who saw possibilities in life and never let any setback derail them. As a result, they all became tremendous successes. This is just a short list, though. There are countless examples of people who came from ordinary beginnings and achieved extraordinary things—in business, in science, in the community, in their lives.

Right now, you are already doing something extraordinary by taking control of your finances. Probably, along the way, you've experienced some of those setbacks. I hope you didn't give up. If you did, change your mind and start again. The only thing that has the power to separate you from success is giving up.

It's Not About Genius, Either

So, you know by now that you don't have to be born rich to become financially successful. It's about discipline. If you follow the steps laid out here in EDED, you will achieve financial success. But if you're like me and most of the other humans in the world, doubts will creep up. *Maybe I'm not worthy of the life I'm dreaming of. Maybe I'm not smart enough.*

But here's the thing: it's not about smarts, either. You don't have to be a prodigy to have the life of your dreams. Achieving financial freedom will build a bridge from where you are today to the life you're dreaming of living. You already know all of the steps to EDED:

- Assess honestly where you are right now.

- Set financial goals, short-term, mid-term, and long-term.

- Make a list of debts (the Debt Knockout) and start paying them off, smallest balance to largest.

- Start keeping all receipts and recording them daily in your logbook.

- Set up your 10/20/70 budget and follow it.

- As you pay down debts, start looking for more ways to save.

- Invest your savings so that they can grow.

- Find a financial professional who is prepared to help you succeed in each of the stages of your financial life—Accumulation, Preservation, and Distribution.

- Enjoy your dream retirement—but keep practicing EDED!

Not one of those steps requires any kind of particular smarts. Success in EDED has to do with sticking with the process. That's it. Stick with the EDED program, and you'll erase your debts, fill your savings to overflowing, and build investments that sustain you in retirement.

Do that, and guess what will happen? Other people, ones who haven't yet made the changes you have, will think you're a genius. Or, they might assume you grew up rich, and that's why you have money. And you will know the truth.

FIRST BELIEVE, THEN DO

I always knew, even as a kid, that I wanted to do something more, something other than just maintain the status quo. I didn't know what that "something more" was for a long time, but I knew that whatever it was, it would move me out of the anxious, debt-driven world I grew up in. Ever since then, I've run on a fear of going backward just as much as a desire to move forward.

The point is this: even before I knew what I wanted to do, I knew one thing. I knew that I was a person who wouldn't settle. I would make my life something better. After that, I just took steps in that direction. Those steps added up, and soon it was easy to see that my life was something better. That's what *Every Dime, Every Day* is all about. You bring the belief, and EDED gives you the steps to take. Take those steps every day, and you too will find that you're headed in the direction of your dreams.

BEFORE MOVING ON
TO THE NEXT CHAPTER:

Time for another honest assessment. Where are you with the EDED steps?

- Are you keeping every receipt?

- Are you maintaining your logbook?

- How is that 10/20/70 budget going? Are there areas you're going over? Can you find ways to save more?

- Where do your debts stand?

- Have you found a financial professional who can help you invest your seed money?

- Have you started saving for retirement?

- Have you achieved any of your short-, mid-, or long-term goals? Have any of them changed? Do you need to make adjustments?

Don't stress—just act. Every assessment is just a way to see where you stand and figure out how to stay on track. Your goal is to see the progress you've made and keep moving forward. You were born to succeed, and you will.

Chapter 16:
YOUR FORKS IN THE ROAD

Develop success from failures. Discouragement and failure are two of the surest stepping stones to success.

~ Dale Carnegie

H ere we are, at the end of the book. This is the final chapter, but it's not the end of your journey (or my journey with you) at all. Here's the problem with a book: it has a beginning, middle, and end. It makes it seem like you might start *Every Dime, Every Day*, work through the steps, and then one day finish. But changing your life isn't nearly that simple.

After you reassessed at the end of Chapter 15, where did you find yourself? It's important to know exactly where you are, and to be honest about it, but it's equally important not to let that information stop you from moving forward. If you looked around and found yourself somewhere that looks a lot like the beginning all over again, don't worry about it. Just start where you are and keep going forward.

DISCOURAGEMENT IS LIKE DEBT

Your biggest enemy in the battle for financial wellness is debt. That's because debt is the opposite of wealth. It's like a hole in the hull of your financial ship. But to achieve any goal at all, whether it's financial, personal, spiritual, etc., you have to have hope, and discouragement is the opposite of hope.

How do you battle discouragement then?

Replace the negative. When I was a kid, I was taught that only the rich could get richer. I believed that I, as part of the struggling working class, had no chance. It took me a long time to turn those discouraging voices off. Something that helped, though, was replacing those discouraging voices with ones that I found *encouraging*. Robert Kiyosaki's books were a huge source of hope and inspiration for me, and still are.

If you think I'm the problem, then you have to change me. If you realize that you're the problem, then you can change yourself, learn something, and grow wiser. Most people want everyone else in the world to change but themselves. Let me tell you, it's easier to change yourself than everyone else. ~ Robert Kiyosaki

Try *something*. Over the years, I've had a few forks in the road myself, but the biggest was probably that September morning in 2001 when I discovered that I had invested every penny of our hard-earned savings in a stock market that had just plummeted over a cliff. That was a big fork in the road for sure, and for a few days, I wasn't sure how I would pull together the determination to start over.

I'm not a psychologist, but I've experienced discouragement, and I've talked to people all over the country about their money worries, goals, and dreams. What I've learned is that most of what we consider "failure" is caused by getting discouraged and then giving up. When we have hope, it's like fuel. It makes it easy to try something new, or to try again when something doesn't work. When we get discouraged, that hope energy isn't there. It's not so easy to just start over or pick ourselves up and carry on. That's when we need some strategies to call on, something we can just do, whether we believe in it or not. Because as soon as you start moving again, you'll find that every step gets easier and easier.

It is not work that kills men; it is worry. Work is healthy; you can hardly put more upon a man than he can bear. Worry is the rust upon the blade. It is not the movement that destroys the machinery but the friction.

~ Henry Ward Beecher

Let's say you've been working toward financial freedom. You've been paying down debt and keeping your logbook. But a sudden crisis occurs before you've got your emergency fund in order. Maybe you lose your job or someone you love gets sick. You feel overwhelmed and discouraged. What are your choices? Do you accept that you will be in debt forever? That doesn't do you any good. But it's not easy to get back on the horse after being bucked off, either. So why not choose one thing you can do that will help your situation? You could sell something and use the proceeds to pay some of your debt. You could look through your logbook and find just a little more money you could save in your budget. Anything you choose will help because it will get you moving forward again, and that's what really matters.

Find inspiration. Every struggling person needs an example of someone else who also struggled and overcame. That's why I'm writing this book. I know how important it is to learn the stories of people who succeeded, and I want every person who dreams of financial freedom to know that it is possible, no matter your background. My story is just one of many, though, and you should be aggressive about finding more examples that inspire you.

You can't wait for inspiration.
You have to go after it with a club.

~ Jack London

Books are a great way to find inspiration, but you can also find some great and motivating success stories on blogs and podcasts. I've included some of my favorite sources of inspiration at the back of this book, but don't stop there. Achieving financial freedom is difficult. If it wasn't, everyone would do it! For that kind of challenge, you need fuel, and inspiration is exactly the fuel you need.

Help someone else. Wherever you are in life, whatever your challenges, there is always someone else you can help. Is there a person at your work who could use a hand or some positive feedback? A kid you know who could use a mentor? A charity in need of a volunteer? When you help someone else be successful, you remind yourself of all the talents and gifts you have to offer. If you're feeling low or overwhelmed, there's nothing more empowering than taking your focus off yourself and putting it on someone else in need.

You have not lived today until you have done something
for someone who can never repay you.

~ John Bunyan

Find a mentor. I've said it before, but remember this: when the student is ready, the teacher appears. John was one of my many mentors, and the effect he has had on my life is immeasurable. So how do you find your mentor? First, look around you. You might already know your mentor or even be working with your mentor, as I was with John, and not know it.

My mentor happened to work in insurance, which is related to the field I work in now, but I didn't know at the time that I was going to work in finance. When I met John, all I knew was that I needed a career that offered more opportunity for advancement and income. Insurance sales sounded like a good possibility, and even though it wasn't the path for me at that time, John's influence transformed my outlook.

When you look around, don't be critical. Don't weed people out based on your expectations. Simply consider the people you know, work with, go to church with, etc. and think about which ones you admire. Who has something to teach? Whose life already embodies some of the most important goals you have for yourself? That's a person who can help you along your way.

A mentor is someone who allows you to see the hope inside yourself.

~ Oprah Winfrey

WHAT TO DO NEXT:

There's no "what to do before moving on to the next chapter" because you've arrived—not at the end of your journey, just at the end of this book. The most important thing you can do now, as I've mentioned a few times already, is keep moving forward. Don't let discouragement or setbacks or forks in the road stop you. Even if they slow you down, even if they push you back for a bit, pick up and move forward again as quickly as you can.

Sometimes, though, it can be difficult to tell if you're moving forward at all. That's why, as a final step in this book, I will ask you to make a new habit. Every month, when you are reconciling your bank statements with your logbook, do one more thing: take a look at your goals. Some of your goals are mid-term and long-term, so you might not have achieved them yet, but you can assess where you are in the process. Are you still moving forward? And just as importantly, check in with your short-term goals. Which ones have you achieved? When you cross one of your goals off, any of your goals, reward yourself. Celebrate. You are changing your life and the lives of everyone you love. You are doing something amazing, and the amazing things you do, if you stay on this path, are only going to get better.

So, celebrate, keep moving forward, and keep in touch. I will be thrilled to hear about your journey.